MARKETING TECHNIQUES FOR
ANALYSIS AND CONTROL

Marketing Techniques for Analysis and Control

Peter Allen
B.Sc. (Econ.), A.M.B.I.M., A.M.I.S.M., M.B.I.M.A., M.I.Ex.

MACDONALD AND EVANS

MACDONALD & EVANS LTD.
Estover, Plymouth PL6 7PZ

First published 1977

©
MACDONALD AND EVANS LIMITED
1977

ISBN: 0 7121 1394 0

Printed in Great Britain by
Latimer Trend & Company Ltd Plymouth

Preface

Since 1945 there have been great changes in the concept of business operations of which the most significant factor has been the rise of the marketing function.

Before the Second World War, business in Europe, and to a lesser extent in the United States, was dominated by the ability of production. In a world which was beset by economic problems of recession, unemployment and falling living standards, firms had little incentive to innovate; after all, "people were lucky to get anything" seemed to be the overall philosophy. Lord Keynes's concept of governmental intervention seemed to change all that and in the years since 1945 the Western world has had unparalleled growth and an apparently endless ability to produce and absorb output. Perhaps in retrospect we may see that there were forces at work which only gave the impression of economic control, rather than the reality. In those years of reconstruction, manpower shortages and low unemployment, the economic boom provided an environment in which the marketing concept came to replace the older production-oriented ideas of business.

The marketing concept which "matched total company resources to product/market opportunity" saw the consumer as the most important element in the complex inter-reacting structure of business and so he was—so long as he was employed and confident. In the years of growth between the early 1950s and the early 1970s marketing succeeded, but in such a climate of opportunity it might have been difficult for it to fail.

In the autumn of 1973, a realisation that we were overstretching our finite resources came to a head. Oil became the critical factor and with its escalation in price came incredible imbalances of trade, rampant inflation, mounting unemployment and a realisation that the concept of governmental contra-cyclical action to control the economy was not working.

Now marketing is to be tested. Can it in time of difficulty continue to stimulate business as it did in times of economic growth? The answer probably is that we are better off under-standing the role of marketing and consumer behaviour than we would be with a purely production-oriented system of out-put. But marketing must seek to be a more exacting function. The intuition and judgment, the creativity and persuasion must now be tempered with hard facts, measurable facts to reduce the business risk as much as possible. In marketing the risk cannot be completely removed but if it can be significantly reduced then we may yet survive.

For nearly seventy years techniques have existed that have found their application in production and since World War Two, new techniques of analysis have emerged. The aim of this book is to relate these techniques to the marketing function so that its task can be made less unpredictable.

This book is the result of marketing lectures given to H.N.D. Business Studies groups, and to courses for the Diploma in Management Studies. It will provide in one book much of the knowledge needed for those taking the final examinations of these courses as well as those studying for the Diploma in Marketing, Diploma in Industrial Marketing, the Institute of Export and a wide range of management and business courses in Polytechnics, Colleges and Universities.

I would like to acknowledge and thank those companies which have allowed me to quote examples of their experiences, including English China Clays Sales Company Ltd., Avana Group Ltd., and Strads International Ltd. I would also like to acknowledge the permission given by Tavistock Publications Ltd. for the use of Fig. 23, from their publication, *O.R. Comes of Age*, edited by Rolfe C. Tomlinson.

Feb. 1977   P.A.

Contents

List of Illustrations

List of Tables

CHAPTER ONE

Applying marketing techniques

Changing role of marketing

The need for a book on the application to marketing of analysis and control arises out of the rapidly changing business environment. In the Preface to this book it has been suggested that marketing has been successful so far during a fairly lengthy period of economic growth, low unemployment and confidence among consumers. In these circumstances marketing evolved to exploit increasing demand from consumers eager to differentiate their purchases.

In the early stages of an expansion in consumer demand there is room for companies to manoeuvre, to try new ideas, new promotions, new designs and new methods of selling to consumers. But, as with any other situation where a single variable, in this case the customer, is influential for many other variables, an element of diminishing returns must eventually arise. Customers who have been persuaded to buy cars, domestic appliances, holidays and so on, must become progressively more discerning and marginal in their response to marketing appeals, especially for replacement products. The car will have to last another year, the holiday is postponed and clothes handed down. That situation is greatly exacerbated if it happens to coincide with social pressures such as environmental considerations, and economic pressures typified by a growing awareness of the limitations of raw materials, sources of energy and foodstuffs.

In the mid-1970s we have a situation in which all the aforementioned factors have become critical. The question now, then, is what might be the role of marketing in a situation of falling demand and short supply? Both ends of the supply and demand syndrome are under stress for a variety of reasons but the result is the need for companies to consider again their strategy for getting their production consumed.

None of this is to say that marketing as a corporate strategy is going to be replaced by former ideas of a dominant production or sales function. Knowledge of Keynesian economics and methods of creating demand will enable companies to employ their factors of production and their skills in the market place to a much higher degree than in the thirties and hopefully avoid a stagnating policy of only selling what is made.

For marketing to continue as a decisive factor of corporate policy in the much more thrifty economy that is likely to pertain for the foreseeable future, it must on a functional basis, become less of an art and more of a science in its application. This is probably inevitable to a large degree.

Marketing as a functional title evolved from the activities of selling and many marketing men began their careers in sales. Sales-originated personnel invariably have a pragmatic approach to creating customers and are not always receptive to the more theoretical concepts of behaviourism fundamental to marketing.

Marketing is very much a subject for management and business studies and in the process a new kind of marketing person is being created. The marketing man, and woman, of the future will have to fulfil a different role, for the role of marketing itself is changing. The original personnel relied upon a descriptive presentation of information and their assessment was largely qualitative. The growing complexity of business and the increasing competitiveness of the total marketing environment demands that marketing personnel should be competent in the areas of economics, finance, statistics and the behavioural sciences. This does not in any way diminish the managerial role and the handling of complex concepts and data will always need guidance that only comes with experience.

The stricter disciplines of marketing techniques embodied in management science create a proportional demand for higher qualities of leadership and judgment. Management and leadership are different qualities and while we hear a great deal of the former, leadership is regrettably not stressed enough.

The task of marketing management is intellectual and may be summarised in three ways:

1. Formulation of policy.
2. Decision-making within the framework of policy.
3. Provision of facilities for implementing policies.

These three areas of policy, decision-making and implementation necessitate the provision of information. A field commander faced with the same three needs cannot, in the absence of adequate intelligence, choose the best strategy and neither can a marketing manager. Marketing, like warfare, has moved into the electronic era, when decisions flash as computer outputs in response to inputs, but as has been remarked, "rubbish in—rubbish out." The rapid pace of change in the business environment calls for better responses in terms of a greater state of awareness of what *might* happen; logical responses when it *does* happen; and if possible a larger element of *control* in the event itself.

Marketing management is working in an environment over which it has only marginal control. Any claim to manipulate its environment can itself only arise out of a clear understanding of that environment's expectations since marketing rides a behavioural pattern rather than creates it. Nevertheless any marketing manager who understands his environment to the extent of being able to predict trends and manipulate his strategy accordingly is strongly placed for success.

The firm and its environment

It is usual to regard the firm as an assortment of facts, figures and persons going about its tasks on a day-to-day basis. In reality the firm is more analogous to a living organism. Kotler has described the firm in its environment as an *ecosystem*, comparing it to the study of ecology which is concerned with living organisms and their relationships to their surroundings. In *Sales and Sales Management*, Macdonald & Evans, 1973, I suggested: "An organism, to survive, has to be capable of adaption —a process of change by which it modifies itself to a form better suited to the evolving environment." Referring again to the work of Kotler, he defined the marketing environment in these terms: "The environment is the totality of forces and entities that are external and potentially relevant to the particular agent."

A living organism of today has evolved from lower and generally more simple forms of life that have themselves been successful. It is a continual process of struggle leading to what Charles Darwin described as survival of the fittest. How does a living organism survive? It develops facilities and weapons which will suit it best to its surroundings at a particular time. In this it is concerned with defending itself against predators and is also concerned with providing for its needs in terms of survival. If the environment in which it lives changes significantly then the organism must modify its way of life.

There is a species of moth in Britain which in the heavily industrialised regions of its range has adapted to a melanistic form. This has been an adaptation to survival in a habitat where the trees on which it lives have themselves become darkened by industrial pollution. A pale-coloured moth is easily seen against a dark background and any light specimens are soon eaten by predators. In the rural habitats the reverse is true.

Firms must also modify the way they behave in response to their environment. Firms which sell abroad will not be successful unless they modify to their new surroundings. A moth which is the wrong colour dies, a firm with the wrong set of responses or attributes also dies. Fortunately the process is not so quick or final as it is for the moth, otherwise there would be few firms left. But it is true to say that the environment is changing much more rapidly at the present time and the business world is experiencing a period of upheaval as inflation, unemployment and politics introduce new circumstances into the environment, and frequently new rules as well. Just as the organisms which survive physical upheavals are stronger and fitter, so the firms which survive should be stronger. Rightly or wrongly, society will no longer let all weak firms die and so many firms, and even industries, remain to be basically unviable and have to be subsidised, a form of existence not yet evident in the natural world.

Management science has a significant contribution to make in aiding the firm's survival in this *ecosystem*. Firms have an advantage over organisms in the natural world in that they are able to investigate their environment, any likely changes that might occur and predict what modifications are necessary.

Business firms exist in order to fulfil the needs of the environment in which they operate at a particular place and time.

They are not static enterprises but as we have already seen are dynamic and resemble living organisms in their pattern of survival, which is a reaction to their environment. This reaction is a response to stimuli by which they experience the need for change and as a result of changes in technology, markets, economic and political changes and changes in the legal framework. If it is to survive, the firm must respond to these stimuli in one of two ways, and sometimes both:

1. It will modify the environment through its communications, public relations or marketing activities, including advertising and the sales force; or

2. respond by its own adaptations undertaken as a reaction to an identifiable need for change (*see* Fig. 1).

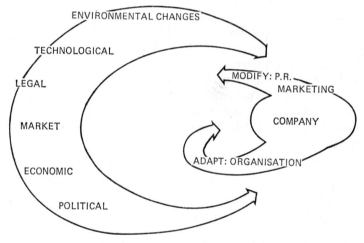

FIG. 1.—*The environment and the factors of change.*

Between the stimuli and the reaction will be the decision process which will have determined the nature of the reaction.

The initial response to change will be constructing the correct organisation structure to deal with the new situation. Most organisation is, in reality, a process of re-organisation in response to the changing needs, and the marketing manager given the task of examining the suitability and the logic of existing structures is essentially concerned with re-organisation. Only a minority of organisational changes appear to result from innate discontent with the existing organisation structure. Joan Woodward's studies of firms suggested that such changes occurred as a consequence either of changes in top management or a growing awareness of the need for organisation by the chief executive. Generally the increased consciousness was stimulated by exterior contacts, such as attending a senior management course, or introducing management consultants. The study further suggested that organisational changes were not deliberately planned, but rather occurred spontaneously in response to a crisis or to accommodate individuals. Firms' studies showed that, to some extent, organisation had been modified to accommodate individual "empire-builders," who had introduced a distortion in the organisation by their acquisition of higher status.

In this way the marketing company accords to the organisational behaviour of most profit-centred organisations. In *Sales and Sales Management* I expressed this dynamic influence on the marketing company thus: "A businessman, or a salesman, within his chosen career may move from one organisation to another and is able to advance by his personality and ability, and his willingness to shoulder additional responsibility. Nothing so encourages promotion as a person's willingness to take on extra work." The limitations to this "empire-building" will be:

1. The diminishing effectiveness of the individual; and
2. the ability of colleagues to influence or resist this "empire-building."

Creating logical organisation structures is a management planning task and is fundamental to sound business decision-making. For the marketing manager the task is a constantly recurring problem since sales forces are among the first areas of business structures to be modified in response to changing policies within the company or its environment. This area of decision-making is dealt with in Chapter 2 in more detail since here we are concerned with organisation in relation to the marketing environment.

It will be apparent that the marketing environment is a very complex one in which change itself is the only certainty. To cope with the many areas of uncertainty is in itself a difficult task but it is made even more hazardous by the nature of the change and nature of business. While change is becoming more rapid the methods of production and even of marketing are increasingly complex and require longer periods in which to implement changes.

Modern methods of mass-production are usually automated to a higher degree and require lengthy production runs to be viable propositions and to repay the initial capital investment. Marketing effort is organised accordingly and if the product is sold through sophisticated distribution systems by specialist sales or advertising strategies, these too may be difficult to adapt in the short term. Under these increasing pressures marketing has sought more sophisticated techniques of predicting future needs with a higher degree of certainty.

The search for solutions

Marketing techniques are scientific tools of analysis and control to aid managers in solving marketing problems. Their objective is to provide a systematic body of knowledge that will enable management to take better decisions. The needs of marketing management creates the demand for science in the field of marketing.

Marketing management in the usual course of their work delegate authority to subordinates to ensure that work gets done. To take decisions managers obtain information and advice which will, hopefully, enable them to make a good choice.

Marketing techniques extend this general principle of delegation to the *delegation of analysis* and it becomes a different way of dealing with marketing problems requiring the use of techniques not generally employed by the departmental specialist. The use of such techniques necessitates an interdisciplinary approach which usually includes mathematics, operational research, statistics, psychology, sociology, economics, management accounting, systems engineering and computer techniques. These are all fairly conventional disciplines in business but on occasion other less obvious studies such as biology and the visual arts may be employed.

When a marketing problem is recognised it is usually passed downwards and labelled as being financial, distribution, production, etc. In applying the marketing techniques of management science a problem is accepted as not being totally soluble within the confines of a single department. Applying marketing techniques creates the need for an interdisciplinary expertise in which the scientist expects to find what he requires to know of specific functions as a need arises in the process of specific problem-solving. Thus in dealing with a product replacement problem it may be necessary to draw on knowledge from production, design, research and development, finance and costing, marketing and economic research, psychological and sociological sources, distribution and packaging experts.

Marketing techniques begin with attempts to measure in areas which are not usually considered measurable, but management is becoming increasingly aware that it needs data of all kinds to manage effectively. Management accounting and work study are two aids to management that have become accepted and both can be potent aids to marketing.

Management accounting investigates profit and loss in detail, differentiating between a product's cost and its value, revenue earned and cash flows.

"Work study is the term used to describe those techniques employed in the examination of work, and the systematic factors affecting efficiency and economy in a situation, in order to achieve improvement."

Outline of Work Study and Payments by Results,
T.U.C., 1969.

Both techniques are fundamental means of measuring effort and performance against standards and aid marketing in effectively implementing policies. While a manager may determine patterns in the business environment which guide him in the control of that part for which he is responsible, the application of marketing techniques calls for a continual devising of new methods of measuring what, at the time, may be imponderables. Too often in marketing we measure processes while in reality the important activities are not concerned with processes but with data needed to formulate policy, make decisions and devise and implement controls.

Marketing is an area of business that has been too long dominated by value judgments or hunches based on experience. The role of marketing techniques in this area is to determine what factors are causal to a situation and to devise means of measuring them. Marketing techniques, then, must concern themselves with incorporating their findings in quantitative terms into an explanation of the system, why it works as it does and how the system is sustained. At this point the activity of measuring is no longer adequate as frequently we have to find something measurable and to do this we have to employ operational research.

The use of operational research is dealt with in Chapter 4 but it is helpful to understanding the role of marketing techniques if we can see the range of marketing problems to which different but parallel disciplines may be applied.

1. Advertising problems—psychologists, sociologists, mathematicians, economists.

2. New product evaluation—design specialists, engineers, economists, statisticians, management accountants.

3. Pricing strategies—cost analysts, economists, computer experts, statisticians.

4. Environmental studies—sociologists, psychologists, economists, legal experts, statisticians.

Teams of experts such as these *expand* the views of problems in situations where the traditional functional expert has a tendency to narrow the problem. They are a step removed from the day-to-day problems and bring to bear a new approach which may be exemplified by the nine-dot puzzle in Fig. 2. The

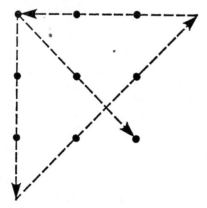

FIG. 2.—*The nine-dot puzzle.*

problem is to join all nine dots with four straight lines while keeping pen to paper. The solution is to go *outside* the problem, yet few people seem ever to do this as their horizons are limited.

Marketing techniques are aids to marketing management and the dialogue begins with marketing management explaining the nature of the problem and how they would be willing to measure performance and implement controls. It is important at this stage that there should be a dialogue so that the problem is defined correctly. Too often management concerns itself with analysing symptoms rather than the actual problem. The symptoms of an advertising problem are poor response in terms of purchases by consumers but to understand the problem may require examination of all the factors involved. Corrective measures may have to be applied in any, or to some degree, all stages in the process.

1. The advertisement itself may be wrong.
2. Media selection may be poor.
3. The advertisement may be seen at the wrong time.
4. Competitors' activity may be too strong.
5. Distribution or display may be inadequate.
6. Pricing may be out of line with the competition.
7. Packaging may be wrong.
8. Economic factors may be affecting sales.
9. There may be something wrong with the product.

It is imperative that the right questions are asked at the outset. When the problem has been agreed upon the next stage is to determine an objective in terms of performance. This dialectical process ensures that manager and management scientist understand what is going on in order to improve the operation, to optimise some process or activity or to suggest alternative ways of achieving the objective. Fig. 3 illustrates steps in the application of marketing techniques to a problem such as the advertising response situation referred to earlier.

Such a model aids marketing management in observing the working of a real-life situation and in producing a hypothesis from which deductions can be made. A general expression of the conditions is expressed as $P = f(C_i\ U_j)$ where P is a measure of performance, or behaviour; f is the function of which C_i is a set of factors under a manager's control; U_j other sets of factors which are independent of management's control.

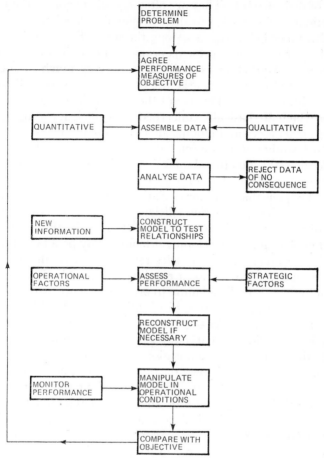

FIG. 3.—*Steps in applying marketing techniques.*

Market planning

In the modern marketing-oriented company the marketing plan lies at the heart of the total company planning process. Decisions on what to produce and what finance will be needed hinge on marketing management's expectations and understanding of customer demand. Yet many companies develop their marketing plans in almost total ignorance of the real market situation and have only vague notions of the shape and size of their markets. They are often equally vague on the likely reactions of the market to their proposed strategies.

Consumer behaviour is among the more difficult subjects to analyse and therefore presents problems in predicting reactions or trends. Marketing as a discipline is very much about behaviour and therefore marketing decisions are very difficult to take with certainty. This is not the case with production decisions which are basically concerned with efficiency in the use of plant, machinery and labour, all areas suited to the application of work study and measurement.

Because the functional plans' effectiveness throughout the company are dependent on the accuracy of marketing plans, it often happens that a minor deviation of sales performance from forecast renders production efficiencies meaningless by virtue of the disruption cost incurred. The cost of maintaining an adequate research and development facility may be allowed for in pricing products. A fall in sales revenue may result in inadequate funds to provide for a continuing research and development budget. Equally a failure to provide a competitive product range, or to utilise the best distributive channels will limit the effectiveness of the sales organisation.

It is a function of marketing plans to encourage congruent goals throughout the organisation and avoid different departments working to their own narrow objectives, often pulling in different directions. Among small companies resources are often so scarce that close consultation and agreement is vital if wastage of effort is to be avoided. A mistake in strategy may result in years of development being wasted.

A small car manufacturer developed a fibre-glass car body to which were fitted engines and transmissions bought in from other manufacturers. Their design was modern and much in demand but competition and their limited marketing policy prevented their pricing the car realistically. All went well for a number of years until other car designs caught up with them, and then overtook. Unfortunately their pricing structure had not permitted their setting aside finance for further development and when sales began to fall in the face of competition, there were no reserves to produce new designs and the firm eventually failed.

In larger companies the problem is combating what J. K. Galbraith called the "technostructure," in which decisions are taken by groups. Such decision-making is slow and tends to reflect the views of members of the group rather than a logical process based on marketing research and forecasting. Frequently conflict arises from the functional origins of the group. Research and development personnel favour a high rate of technical innovation while marketing personnel will seek to attain a high growth rate and expanding markets.

In marketing-oriented companies co-ordination between conflicting and competing activities is attained in two ways:

1. In the matching of total company resources to customer service and marketing opportunity.

2. In the formal organisational grouping of related activities to ensure the optimum use of resources, product planning, financial control and the total distribution system, together with marketing research, promotions and selling.

Co-ordination, if it is to be effective, must be supported by systematic information feedback enabling performance to be monitored and verified by reference to a standard, such as budgeting control. This feedback will highlight failures to attain predetermined and agreed levels of performance and make the subsequent correction more certain.

Much of the control system in marketing is financial since this reduces all standards and performances to a common denominator. Marketing techniques introduce systems of financial analysis which are designed to provide continuous, systematic data as a means both of maintaining a record of present activity and performance and for setting future objectives and standards. This topic is further developed in Chapter 7.

Measuring the problem

Finally in this chapter we shall look at another management technique the purpose of which is to aid understanding of a situation and provide a means of quantification; this is the technique of method study.

"Method study is the application of a logical procedure of investigation, in a form suited to the situation being studied."
Outline of Work Study and Payments by Results,
T.U.C., June 1963.

Method study is a branch of work study and was developed

principally by the Gilbreths in the United States. As a technique it can be applied to a single person, operator, clerk, delivery man, packer or salesman, or to the operations of an entire system. It is based on six principal stages in the process of analysis and improvement.

1. Select the work to be studied;
2. record the facts;
3. examine the facts;
4. develop the new method;
5. install the method;
6. maintain the new method.

Method study aims to establish performance ratings which become the standard against which actual performance can be compared. Its application to marketing and the degree of precision aimed for will depend upon the task being studied. Some, like packaging and documentation, are capable of being reduced to a "best" method and a standardised performance. Others, like the sales force and advertising, will be subject to too many variables and individuality for standard ratings, but nevertheless can benefit from the analytical approach and the resulting better understanding of the process. Method study has a place in marketing and can be justified as a tool of analysis in terms of productivity and efficiency in the use of resources. It is examined more thoroughly in Chapter 10.

In this chapter several techniques of analysis have been introduced which can be applied to problem solving and improving performance. The marketing environment has been explained as a living, dynamic system constantly changing. To survive in this environment firms must be capable of analysing what is happening and take the correct decisions.

CHAPTER TWO

Decision-making

In Chapter 1 it was determined what constitutes a business, the problems it faces in today's conditions and the way it is affected by and reacts with its environment. It is now necessary to develop the concepts further and determine the relationships between the environment, the functional organisation of the company, especially the marketing function, and the needs for decision-making.

In all business management there is a prime responsibility to allocate resources and their utilisation. Having determined the disposition of resources, it is necessary to assess the outcome of applying them in particular ways. Marketing management is responsible for applying judgment decisions in formulating plans and for the necessary feedback of information, enabling a control of performance and progress. To achieve the optimum in decision-making the marketing manager needs data derived from information on economics, physical and financial resources. The feedback of information enables the decision-maker to be rational in selecting a course of action.

The decisions that are required to ensure efficiency of operation may be either routine day-to-day or weekly activities that a marketing manager is responsible for, or may require major action to be taken. These latter decisions will usually be non-recurring and relate to situations of importance in which an error of judgment may result in the need for correction at considerable cost. It is important to decision-making that the information needs and available data must be appropriate to the level of importance of the decision. This situation is typified by the problem of exploring an export market.

A company seeking a market in a country of limited potential may well find that the cost of marketing research will be so costly that it exceeds the short-term potential. In the long term the potential may not exist at all if there is a latent instability in the country. Fig. 4 illustrates the relationships between the cost of obtaining the information as determined by the cost of permitting errors to arise.

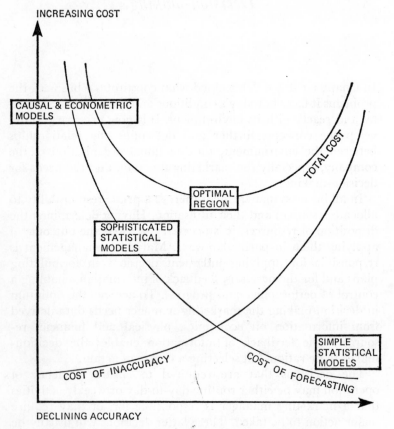

FIG. 4.—*The cost of obtaining information and the cost of research.*
(a) *Cost and accuracy increase with sophistication and may be charted against the corresponding cost of forecasting errors.*
(b) *The most sophisticated technique that can be economically justified is one that falls in the region where the sum of the two costs is minimal.*

Decision-making in business is entwined with four principal areas which in turn are paramount to the functional organisation of the business as shown in Fig. 5. Marketing, as the most

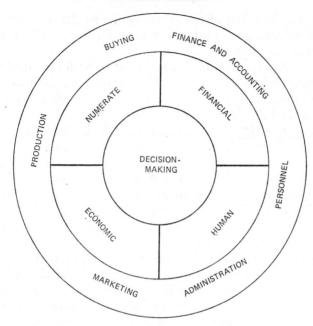

Fig. 5.—*Four principal decision areas.*
The relevant functions are also shown.

dynamic of the functions of business, is especially concerned with understanding these areas.

Economic decisions

Economics is essentially concerned with choice and determining the way in which choice is made between various alternatives. It is concerned with making sure that the firm uses its available resources in the best possible way so as to benefit the total function rather than any single part of it. Economic analysis in decision-making will examine and evaluate all the possibilities open to the manager, even the more remote. In economics the principal consideration is in terms of the forgone benefits as "opportunity" costs. The economist measures cost not in terms of using £1,000 for using a resource, say advertising, but rather the cost of not being able to use that £1,000 for an alternative purpose such as the annual sales conference, or on a new training programme. The cost of the advertising being, in real terms, the inability to have the sales conference. Any decision in these

terms will be taken after evaluating the results of using a resource for a range of purposes and considering the effects of an
action on the major decision need.

Economics is fundamental to business but for marketing in
particular it is the basis of decision throughout the functional
organisation. It is also the environment in which marketing
operates and therefore underlies all strategic decisions relating to
the firm and to its environment. Economics is vital to marketing
decisions since marketing is itself an extension of economics and
may be considered the operational end of the economic spectrum.
All marketing decisions are based on economic considerations—
pricing policy and promotion are both dependent on an understanding of elasticity of demand, selling and distribution are
built on the theory of value and the creation of consumer or
industrial demand derives from an understanding of marginal
utility and the relationships between wants and utility.

Other wider decisions also depend upon the allocation of
resources and the ways in which the factors of production are
combined. For example, the decisions that have to be taken
relating to mass-production and economies of scale. On the one
hand mass-production confers benefits of economies of scale
which has led to the general availability of a wide range of
consumer goods enabling the creation of mass-consumption.
But against these advantages have to be set the social problems
of standardisation of products and the monotony of work that
affects workers. Economics is at the basis of decisions relating
to manpower and wages, availability of capital and the choice
of investments. All business decisions involve choice and can
only be measured on the basis of the costs involved. These are
represented in Fig. 6.

The alternative solutions will each be subject to a cost
analysis. The financial cost will be the actual cost to the company of an action. As mentioned above the opportunity cost is
a peculiarly economic consideration in terms of the cost of
sacrifice. Finally the social cost, or community cost, which, in
large companies in particular, is the effect a course of action
may have on the community and that will in turn affect the
way the community regards the firm. It happens on occasion
that an innovation producing economies of scale will have a
detrimental effect if the result is an unfavourable reaction from
the market due to increased unemployment.

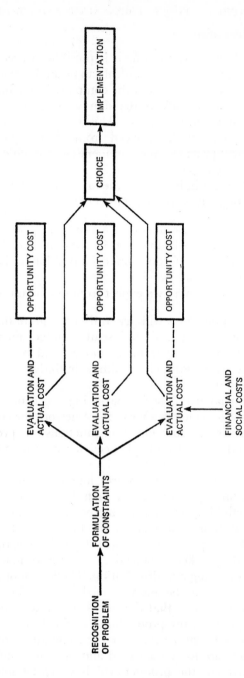

Fig. 6.—*Economics in decision-making.*

Financial decisions

From an analysis of past results it is possible to predict likely future occurrences. Financial control can be analysed to provide some guidance on the direction the company is moving in and, most important, to identify the decisions which need to be taken to make progress more certain. This requires a plan to be formalised which will be derived from an analysis of past results. This will provide a measurement against which current progress can be compared.

Financial control in looking to the future seeks definable and quantitative objectives. It seeks answers to:

1. What financial results do we aim for?
2. What costs will be involved in attaining the objectives?
3. How will this affect our financial position in six months' time, or a year's time?
4. What return may we expect from our investment?

The financial decisions will generally necessitate the process of determining a budget. To be useful a budget must express the aims and controls in terms of money and be capable of analysis in a way that neither limits initiative nor permits wastage of resources.

Many financial decisions in marketing are centred on the product life-cycle which is a natural framework for control. In particular it brings together the functions of production, marketing and finance and the need for co-ordinated planning.

Any product innovation requires long-term investment in terms of capital expenditure, raw materials, promotional and marketing activities. The return to the investment has to be predicted at different times of the product life-cycle, which is illustrated in Fig. 7. The return will depend upon the attainment of specific marketing objectives in terms of market share and the cost of selling and distribution. The length of time over which the product can be sold will need to be predicted so that the firm can make sure that the heavy investment in research and development, pre-production engineering and pre-marketing activity can be recovered at some future date.

If these costs are to be recovered and the fixed and variable costs also covered, the product will have to be sold over a lengthy period of time. The ability to achieve these sales may be limited by competitive activity or lack of continuing capital. It will also involve production decisions on the optimum plant to obtain a certain output at a given cost, the buying of raw materials and resources. All such functional questions have financial involvement which will be resolved in financial decisions on the return to capital employed. At any one time a company may have a number of projects under consideration. The company will wish to know if the investment yield to its project will be at least as good as the company is obtaining with its existing investment, or any alternative projects. This important concept is dealt with further in relation to international marketing.

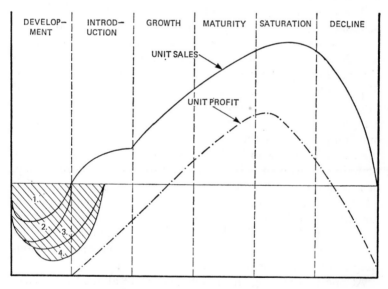

FIG. 7.—*Product life-cycle and recovery of investment.*
Costs: 1. Research. 2. Engineering.
3. Pre-production. 4. Pre-marketing.

Human relations decisions

So far the areas discussed are non-personal. They have been related to choice, costs and financial return methods, which have considered the use of resources. All firms need resources which they obtain from the factors of production, *i.e.* land, labour, capital and enterprise. The measurements discussed have been in the main concerned with the factor of resources; it is necessary now to consider the human element, which is present in the factors of labour and enterprise. The latter include management as a skill and a social practice.

The early management pioneers, notably F. W. Taylor, identified man with the machine and endeavoured to manipulate the worker in the same way as a machine; something to be examined in detail, pre-determined and planned to fit the needs of his function. The needs of mass-production dictated that jobs should be simple and repetitive. While this has enabled great economies of scale to be achieved, it has also led to social problems resulting from monotony and frustration.

There is a large amount of evidence to show the incidence of monotony and frustration on the shop floor and this well might be thought a disease of production. But this complaint is undoubtedly present to a large extent in marketing, in particular among sales people in companies that treat salesmen as dispensable order-takers who have to be directed and coerced to put forth adequate performance. There is ample evidence of a high turnover in salesmen and a continual movement from one company to another which is usually the result of frustration. A salesman who is given little real responsibility for the planning of his own effort inevitably thinks that more money, or a bigger car at the next job will offset his boredom. This is what in essence Professor Frederick Hertzberg called "jumping for jelly beans." The frustration and the resulting movement from job to job are in many ways better examples of Mac-Gregor's Theory X, work-centred approach to human relations than most shop floor disputes.

At one time during the 1960s there were about twelve electrical wholesalers in South Wales. Each employed a couple of salesmen, who were euphemistically called "representatives." Like so many companies the term "representative" seemed to carry a respectability not afforded "salesman;" there is little doubt it attracted men to the job who would not have liked to have been called "salesman" but that was hardly the way to ensure an enthusiastic approach to the task of selling.

During a period of several years these same men would appear representing different firms within the group of about twelve wholesalers. They would work for a while, learn of marginally better prospects "up the road" and move on. Sometimes they went back again. The wastage in terms of upset, new techniques and settling-in must have been enormous for in actual terms the differences between them all were small.

Marketing management and sales management especially have a great responsibility in the area of human relations decisions. Certainly the manager faced with a major policy decision on a system of compensation or how to improve performance, has to be able to relate the problems of a non-standardised work method and a different method of supervision to the gains of job enlargement.

Numerate decisions

If marketing management is to avoid taking decisions solely on the basis of intuition, judgment and experience, it is important that the variables should be accorded some degree of measurement. In forecasting future demand the company has a number of alternative methods which it can use to attain such an indication:

1. Intuition;
2. extrapolation from previous years' figures;
3. market research into the existing market situation;
4. a combination of all these methods.

Businesses need not operate on the basis of hunches, or by trial and error. Developments in statistics have demonstrated that most progress and prediction can be based on numerical data. This is especially so in the areas of economics and marketing.

Decisions based on figures give better results than those in which hunches play a major role. This has led to an increasing demand for numerate information. It is the role of statistics to ensure that the mass of information is correctly handled, arranged, analysed, communicated to decision-makers and, most important, understood. This may be considered in two parts—*descriptive* methods to handle a large volume of numerate information, and *analytical* methods, the means by which the correct deductions can be drawn from the data.

B

It is not possible to undertake statistical analysis in the absence of information. The collection of the figures is important since any errors in the collection will be carried on into the analytical phase and will be reflected in the conclusions. It is vital that marketing management, when making decisions based on numerate information, remembers that the conclusion is only as reliable as the original information upon which it is based.

Organisation and decision-making

Decisions will have to be taken at all levels in the firm. In the following consideration of organisation we will see how there is a hierarchy of decision-making. All decisions in marketing management will involve to some extent the elements discussed above—economic, financial, human and numerate.

Creating logical organisation structures is a management planning task and is fundamental to sound decision-making. Organisation is defined in the *Principles and Practice of Management*, edited by E. F. L. Brech, as:

". . . the structure of the responsibilities allocated to the managerial, supervisory and specialist positions and of the (formal) relationships that arise in the discharge of those responsibilities."

Another definition, this time by T. T. Paterson in *Management Theory*, states: "The theory of organisation is concerned with the way in which jobs are related with one another in a decision system."

Organisation is all that these definitions make it, but above all else it is concerned with human relationships, for the men who conceive and control the organisation have a considerable influence upon it, and the relationships so formed. There is not room in this book to deal extensively with the fundamentals of organisation theory and readers are recommended to the author's book, *Sales and Sales Management*, Macdonald & Evans, 1973.

Here it is sufficient to stress that organisation structures need to be adapted to the specific requirements of individual companies and it follows therefore that each structure must be developed as the situation demands. What is true of the business as a whole is also true of the marketing function alone.

For sound decision-making people at all levels must be aware of the overall objectives of the marketing organisation and, within that framework, their own personal goals and their responsibilities for attaining them. Organisation structures have to be so designed that it becomes possible for the function to achieve its objective over a period of years. The time period itself will need to relate to company needs extending into the future and will be derived from the company's forecasts. These will explore the future in a search for information, both environmental and internal, about which decisions will need to be taken. Because, in general terms, the problem is implicit in the policy, an understanding of the future will enable the firm to predict likely future needs in time to make the necessary changes.

Decisions on the kind of structure that will be needed to achieve the functional objective is a management planning problem. Peter Drucker, in *The Practice of Management*, identified three specific ways—activities analysis, decision analysis and relations analysis.

Activities analysis derives from the realisation that the activities needed in the functional organisation structure will derive from an analysis of the functional objectives. Thus, if marketing management decides to initiate an export drive, it will need to create an organisation structure which includes expertise in exporting. In the absence of such analysis any functional organisation is evidence of management inertia and will result in non-adaptive structures; the structure must reflect the objective.

To achieve the correct organisation marketing management must decide what has to be done, how it will be achieved, specify who will do it and institute controls to ensure it is done well. This analysis will lead to decisions on activities and their relative importance. Most organisation, as was stated in Chapter 1, is re-organisation, and evidence shows that longer-established firms need such analysis more than the younger firm. A successful company will often develop rapidly and individuals will acquire additional tasks which distort and frequently make the organisation illogical. The analysis will reveal which of the activities have declined in importance, and also the need for emphasis on new and important activities.

Decision analysis proceeds from the realisation that organisation is basically a decision-making system which encompasses the decision-making process. The organisation will provide a rational structure enabling decisions to be carried out correctly. Fig. 8 illustrates a framework for the concept of a decision-making hierarchy.

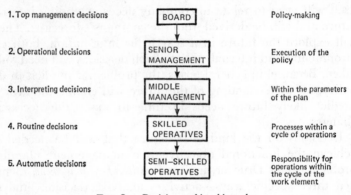

FIG. 8.—*Decision-making hierarchy.*

Such a hierarchy of decisions requires management to identify the level and importance of decision needs and to build into the organisation structure the necessary posts. Since decision-making implies a future reaction it is vital to know who is to take the decisions which will have long-term ramifications and what interactions there will be with other functions. Decisions are like earthquakes, they can be measured by the diameter of their shockwaves.

A marketing decision on the continuance or dropping of a product will have many implications: production will have spare capacity which might affect other costings; sales will have to replace the product's share of the sales-mix with something else and among customers who may buy all their supplies elsewhere if the product is no longer available.

Decisions should always be taken as low as possible in the hierarchy and close to the point of application. Analysing the predictable decision-needs will reveal to management what organisation structure is necessary for the firm and what authority and responsibility must be accorded to each level of management and supervision.

Relation analysis is the final stage in the analytical process following the activities and decisions analyses. A manager controlling a marketing activity will be working closely with other people. An area sales manager will make a contribution to the work of his sales manager and also have work contributed to him by salesmen who are his subordinates. The lateral, or sideways relationships, will bring his activity into contact with other activities at the same level in other functions and he will be in contact with customers. All these needs have to be recognised to be sure that his job is in accord with the functional objectives.

Scientific approach to decision-making

Having examined general ideas on decision-making it is necessary to look at more formalised ideas. The decisions that have been considered hitherto depend upon experience, judgment, intuition and method; only to a lesser degree do they result from the use of scientific principles. There are areas in marketing where decisions can be made more effectively by applying scientific principles to the solving of marketing problems.

The scientific approach introduces logic to problem-solving and provides for evaluation of alternative courses of action. The data that is needed to evaluate alternative strategies is generally referred to as problem-solving communication. A manager's intuition in deciding on a course of action is supplemented by this data obtained from feedback and indicates market responses.

As an example we can consider an executive faced with increased expenditure on promotion by a major competitor. Clearly in such a circumstance he must take some course of action to counter the effect. Any decision should begin with examining the reaction of the customer. Are they aware of the increased promotional activity? He would want to know what brand switching had taken place between his products and those of his rival. Given time to get a feedback from his customers and the market generally he will avoid costly mistakes in predicting consumer reaction.

How the executive reacts will to some extent depend upon how much of a surprise was his rival's campaign. If the campaign proves immediately damaging he may react without waiting to gather information. Data collection is often a long process and underlies the need for continual research to have information available for decision-makers. It is too late when the pressure is on. Continual research provides an insurance against making errors in the day-to-day operations.

Fig. 9 illustrates a scientific problem-solving model. This shows all the various stages and sources of information and its techniques are probably more suited to the market researcher or a person concerned with product development where they are operating to clear-cut objectives needing a rational answer to a predicted question. For the general decision-maker faced with recurring problems the format is likely to be too complex. A simplified scheme is suggested in Fig. 10 and represents a problem-solving model and the selection of a "best" solution.

Models form valuable tools in the visual presentation of information in a logical sequence and since they necessitate the rational thinking out of the entire problem, focus corporate attention on a specific problem.

Improved management decisions

Managing a marketing enterprise is a process of problem-solving and decision-making. It is essential that the manager is able to apply resources to achieve pre-determined objectives. Objectives may be value-based, rational or a combination of both. For a pre-determined objective, say lowering distribution costs, the manager must determine techniques for achieving this as efficiently as possible. It often happens that the real problem is hidden behind a fog of pseudo-problems and symptoms which attract the manager's attention. By using techniques that can quantify problems the manager is obliged to think deeply of the nature of the problem and to bring to bear aids in decision-making.

Business has been dependent upon human judgment, which is itself involved with complex relationships, and too often decisions are based upon imperfect knowledge which encourages intuition rather than rational analysis. This is not to denigrate the value of experience and sound judgment, which are vital to marketing management, but their value can be increased if accompanied by objective measurement of environmental factors.

In common with other business techniques, such as opera-

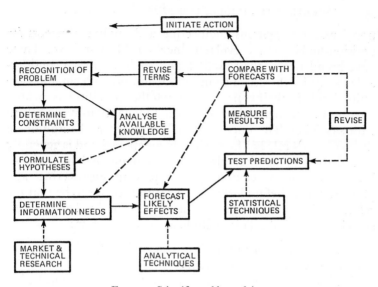

FIG. 9.—*Scientific problem-solving.*

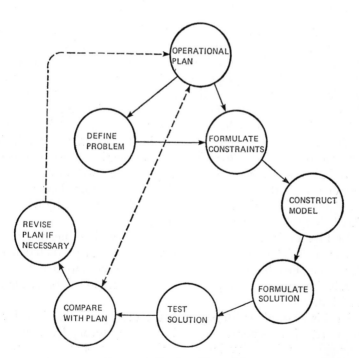

FIG. 10.—*Simple problem-solving.*

tional research, systems engineering and analysis concepts for decision-making have evolved since World War Two. These have broadened in their method and application to a considerable extent by the use of computers. Most of the techniques are quite simple in their concept although the specialist has created an aura about them which causes the manager to regard them with suspicion. The importance of judgment and intuition in the manager's role has been already mentioned and is generally regarded as being the primary decision method in business, leaving the more complex techniques to engineering and physics. The belief underlying this attitude seems to be that the relevant data in business problems cannot be known with sufficient certainty. This attitude omits two factors:

1. Any areas of uncertainty can be identified in advance and allowance made for them.

2. By providing a focus for attention the marketing manager is able to reduce a large and complex problem to a smaller number of significant variables.

Both these factors reduce the area in which judgment is required and removes symptoms that might otherwise attract the manager's attention. In this way decisions on specific issues are more observable. Management should always delegate any decision which can be handled by subordinates and retain only those problems which others cannot take action on.

There is in any problem-solving situation a logical form to be decided. The first stage is to determine the *objective* of the decision. Secondly, any *alternative* courses of action must be specified. Third, it is wise to define the probable *results* of the action together with the interactions with other factors. Fourthly, it must be seen that the objective itself is the criterion by which a choice between alternatives is made.

In Fig. 11 is illustrated the data that will be needed in a *venture-analysis* situation, the estimated cost and predicted performance of each alternative. Table I then seeks to analyse this purely imaginary example in order to provide a basis for a decision.

In this example strategy (A) is the most profitable but does it accord with corporate policy in the long term? Does such a strategy permit a development of other products in a new "industrial cleaner range" market? Strategy (B), while appar-

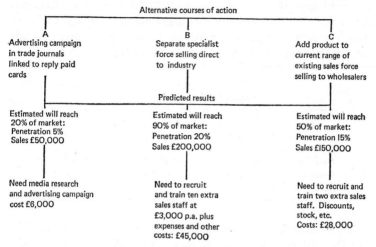

To launch a new industrial cleaner
to obtain within I year a 20% share
of a total market of £I million.

Alternative courses of action

A
Advertising campaign in trade journals linked to reply paid cards

B
Separate specialist force selling direct to industry

C
Add product to current range of existing sales force selling to wholesalers

Predicted results

Estimated will reach 20% of market: Penetration 5% Sales £50,000

Estimated will reach 90% of market: Penetration 20% Sales £200,000

Estimated will reach 50% of market: Penetration I5% Sales £I50,000

Need media research and advertising campaign cost £6,000

Need to recruit and train ten extra sales staff at £3,000 p.a. plus expenses and other costs: £45,000

Need to recruit and train two extra sales staff. Discounts, stock, etc. Costs: £28,000

FIG. 11.—*Venture analysis.*

ently less profitable in the first year of operation, might be more profitable in the longer term, especially if the high launch costs of recruitment and training could be amortised over the life of the product. Expectation lies at the basis of decision theory and is the basic criterion.

To continue this simplified example the firm will make preliminary studies of the market for its industrial cleaner. From

TABLE I. *Cost analysis of alternative strategies.*

Total cost of strategy	Penetration	Sales in £I million	Contribution	Net contribution
(A) £6,000	5%	£50,000	@ 60% £30,000	£24,000
(B) £45,000	20%	£200,000	@ 30% £60,000	£15,000
(C) £28,000	15%	£150,000	@ 25% £37,000	£9,500

this data, the marketing manager can make some estimates of likely profit and loss resulting from achieving different levels of market penetration, as shown in Table II, at 5 per cent, 20 per cent and 15 per cent respectively for the three alternative strategies. In this example it is assumed that the costs of dropping the new product are zero, as development costs will have been written off and are not relevant for this example.

TABLE II. *Level of penetration.*

| | Level of penetration | | |
	20%	15%	5%
Decision	0·5 chance	0·2 chance	0·3 chance
Launch	100	—50	—40
Drop	0	0	0

The marketing manager has predicted the chances of achieving the different levels of market penetration at a fixed price. This simplified example assumes the total of the chances add to unity, that is, indicating all possible variables are included. The basis of decision theory is comparing the anticipated penetration level with an alternative. The choice between alternatives would be based on selecting the penetration level with the greatest expectation. Generally this is known as the *expected monetary value.*

Analysing this example gives an EMV (launch) figure of: $(100 \times 0.5) - (50 \times 0.2) - (40 \times 0.3) = 27$. On the basis of the example with no costs for an option of dropping the product, the decision will be to launch, although there is a 90 per cent chance of the launch not achieving the penetration. In this situation more information is required and the marketing manager will undoubtedly call for assistance from marketing research.

To determine the benefit of such research management will compare the expected monetary value of the optimum decision following research, minus the cost of the research, with the anticipated expected monetary value of the supposed best option before research. The market research data will have been an acceptable expenditure if the expected net gain is greater after research than it was before.

It is helpful to marketing in setting a limit on the value of research to hypothesise what might happen under conditions of perfect information. Bayesian theory asserts that past experience can be combined with existing information to present a decision on a future event. There are costs of delaying a decision and these have to be set against the costs of uncertainty related to a decision without further information.

Decision trees aid the manager in dealing with risk without eliminating it. Perfection in the construction of a decision tree does not make success in the venture a certainty. A decision tree, like other exercises in model-building, is important because it focuses attention on the problem and enables a range of expert knowledge to be applied. A venture analysis such as this allows an expression of doubts as well as opinion. It enables a comparison to be made not only of whether this decision is correct but, over a period of time, whether forecasts compare favourably with the results.

The decision-making process is inseparable from marketing activities. It is essential to projects such as a new product launch, assessing the optimum level of a market research project, competitive pricing policies, investment in new schemes at home and abroad and virtually any other area of doubt.

CHAPTER THREE

International marketing and resource allocation

Appraising international market opportunities

Companies may become interested in international marketing in a number of ways. For most companies it is largely a matter of chance that export orders arrive. Generally these originate as a result of overseas customers finding out in one of several ways:

1. Seeing advertisements in British newspapers, journals or magazines which find their way abroad;
2. by enquiring of British commercial departments abroad, the Department of Trade, trade associations or Chambers of Commerce;
3. by contacting all possible suppliers;
4. as a result of contact with British firms either on a personal basis or by recommendation.

For the company which receives the orders it represents an extension to their markets. It does form an extension into international marketing, but it is a process of exporting.

Exporting is the process of seeking orders abroad by means of an overseas importer, agent, distributor or direct company representation abroad. The system has clear advantages in minimising investment in fixed facilities abroad, although it does raise problems of having to pay tariffs and often experiencing a less favourable reception in the overseas markets. It must be said that where customs unions, such as the European Economic Community, have been established, both these factors have diminished in importance. There still remains, however, problems of transportation.

In this chapter we need to go further than the initial steps of exporting as a means of obtaining a share of international markets. We are also concerned with decisions on international marketing, that is the concept of a truly global corporation.

Management's task in international marketing is complicated by the international aspect of the work and this adds another dimension to the job. There are several major elements of the necessary skills.

The manager must be well experienced in marketing generally and have a thorough understanding of the concepts, tools and techniques to be able to apply them effectively to strategy and tactics abroad. He must also be able to exert the essential skill in managing operations of great complexity in terms of organising, planning, control and co-ordination, frequently dealing with several countries and their problems simultaneously. This requires an ability to delegate work to staff on a regional basis by organising markets as well as people. A single market can be complex enough and demanding of time, but it must be remembered that each overseas market represents one market with its own problems, traditions, peculiarities and methods of doing business. The manager must have an ability to discern market trends in other countries and recognise the needs of individual markets. It calls for direction in the efforts of researchers and care to ensure that effort and time is not wasted in pursuing doubtful potential or markets that are inherently unstable.

While international marketing is essentially no different from domestic markets it is complicated by international laws, economic factors, distance and communication. This creates problems of administering activities across international boundaries.

In some ways the establishment of trading blocs has reduced the total range of international problems but in so doing has imposed new legal liabilities for companies operating internationally. It means that management cannot simply transplant domestic practices to international operations, but must recognise the need to develop the necessary operations in each market.

The broadening of marketing, especially in Europe, by the success of the European Economic Community, has placed a greater emphasis on marketing and management has to realise that selling internationally is no longer an aggressive or expansionary policy, but is now also a defensive policy aimed at protecting its share of the home market.

Many managements regard international marketing with

suspicion, believing it to be less profitable than domestic sales. It very often is less profitable, due to more pressures of competition, distance, etc., but even if that portion of output which is sold abroad is making a smaller profit it is contributing to the firm's total costs. It enables the firm's fixed costs to be spread over a greater volume of production and also enables more research and development by offering a greater potential. From this it will be seen that even if international operations make less profit, they do add to total company income and are an aid to corporate growth. For companies making goods of a seasonal nature, they also permit continual production to be maintained rather than short-time in the off-season, or the cost of carrying stocks. At a time of cash flow problems, overseas selling improves the flow by maintaining customers all year round. It also acts as a cushion against economic troubles. This year it might be there are problems in the home market, next year Europe and so on. In spite of the general world trading problem, it rarely happens that all markets suffer to the same degree at the same time.

It is important that overseas business is not entered into without consideration of the cost problems. A firm should realise the exact nature of the complexities and use techniques to assess the profitability of overseas business and understand how it might affect its related marketing policies. This requires an ability on the part of marketing management to appraise international opportunities.

Investments in international marketing

A decision to embark on a planned entry into an international market must involve a major commitment of company resources in terms of finance and manpower over a period of time. In today's competitive conditions it is no longer possible to export on a casual in–out basis. Many firms, both in Britain and abroad, formerly used export markets as a means of getting rid of surplus production but that is no longer possible for a number of reasons.

There has been an expansion of world trade that has been accelerating over the last ten years as more countries embark upon planned strategies to gain a share. The dissolution of the colonial empires forced many dependent countries to look to their own resources in terms of manpower and raw materials and in turn this has created market opportunities among people perhaps earning regular income for the first time. The spread of communications, particularly television, has aroused interest in consumer products world-wide and since many developing countries cannot import freely, it has led them to produce these goods themselves where possible. The market for clothing is a good example of this trend. Many British manufacturers had substantial markets in Africa in the 1950s and 1960s but as these countries became independent, the manufacture of clothing was an early expansion of home industry. There was a demand for the products and the machinery was not too sophisticated or costly to buy.

At the other end of the spectrum, dumping has become less possible because of the need to plan on a longer basis. This has arisen out of the increased use of automation. Expensive plant has to be fully utilised over as long a period as possible. It is essential in these circumstances that markets are fully re-searched and potential calculated before production is com-menced.

Increased governmental involvement has prompted greater international controls over international business. There is more emphasis on reciprocal trading agreements, especially with the Eastern Bloc and many socialist countries. The prob-lems of international liquidity, aid to countries, and new ap-proaches to trade arising from shortages in essential raw materials and groups of producing countries working together, have all increased the need for a sound understanding of what is going on, and that leaves little scope for the casual exporter.

In these circumstances it simply is not possible to take a short-term viewpoint in any serious international marketing project. To quote from John K. Shiner:

"Everyone, from the chairman and the president down, must agree that the company should enter the overseas trade. This means that all management personnel must be fully in accord with the plan. Permitting a sales manager to try out export trade without having the support of all management is doomed to failure . . . You must not expect quick success in entering an overseas market."

"A Blueprint for Export Success,"
Marketing, January 1963.

Decisions to enter international markets by means of exporting or by some greater involvement, perhaps a limited assembly or an office abroad, have to be viewed as another way of using company resources. Investment in international marketing is an alternative to investing in plant or machinery, although it may lead to that kind of investment at a later date.

There are substantial costs of entry to a new market and these must be looked upon as medium- to long-term capital investments which it is predicted will make some return at a later date. The project should be evaluated therefore on the basis of the anticipated return on that investment and the risks involved.

The choice of entering an international market is a strategic decision and will have a considerable effect upon the company. Strategic decisions have been defined elsewhere as those which affect a company in relation to its environment. Successful international marketing frequently leads to major expansion of the company, but failure can be expensive and sometimes fatal. It must be remembered that the resources which are invested in international marketing are not in any way special, but are the same resources which could be used to extend the factory, buy a major piece of capital equipment, indulge in new technological research or provide a new canteen. If the resources are lost in exporting, then the real cost of the venture is all the other uses which cannot be implemented.

Strategic decision-making involves four steps; these are shown in Fig. 12.

1. *Recognition of the need to take a decision*, is the first step and often it is not an easy one. The need for a decision implies somebody taking the responsibility for action and for its outcome. All too often it is postponed in the hope the problem will go away, but it rarely does. Also the underlying problem is frequently hidden by a fog of symptoms which can waste a

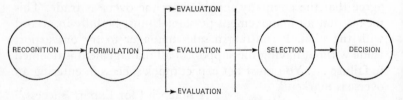

FIG. 12.—*Strategic decision-making.*

great deal of management expertise until it is accepted that they are not causal to the problem.

2. *Formulation of alternatives* is the next and logical step in solving the problem. Just as the problem may have many facets so the solution is unlikely to be too obvious; if it was then there would be no problem. Generally a problem has several possible solutions and it is only after consideration that the best, which may not be the easiest or cheapest, is discovered.

3. *The evaluation of the alternatives* will be the means by which a reasonable solution will be selected. It may be based upon financial, economic or human criteria.

4. The final stage will be the *selection of alternative solutions for a decision.* In the case of international marketing this may be in terms of selecting particular countries or products. It may also involve several different ways of penetrating a market, or indeed the company may abandon the idea altogether if the problems can only be solved at too high a cost.

The traditional method of taking a business decision of this nature is in terms of capital investment theory. Capital investment theory is a valid measure of a project once the first two stages have been determined. The criteria of the return on the investment will aid the evaluation and selection process once the initial steps have been decided. While we can assess the potential of international marketing by this method it is really an incomplete means of initiating the search. Here we are concerned with a determined strategy and want a technique for evaluating an existing project.

There are a number of factors a businessman must consider before taking a decision on investment.

1. Will it be profitable? This is expressed in terms of the relationship between the return to the investment and its cost.

2. The most important consideration of the investment is that the return is to be some time in the future, the creation of goods or future wealth.

3. The state of demand at the present time is the main influence on the businessman's estimate of future profitability; the relationships are shown in Fig. 13.

4. The cost of the investment will determine the prospective return to the investment and this will be dependent upon the rate of interest that has to be paid on the capital borrowed and the opportunity cost of the chosen investment.

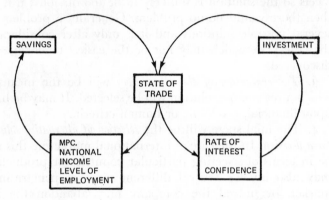

FIG. 13.—*State of trade.*

Confidence is perhaps the most difficult value to quantify but in terms of investment is a key factor. Unfortunately it is a paradox that investment is needed when business is slumping and confidence is at its lowest ebb. Internationally the problem may not be quite the same. If activity at home is low and investment prospects poor, it may be a good opportunity to invest abroad.

Determining the approach

A consideration of actual cost and the opportunity cost suggests a framework for evaluation and decision-making for market entry. It also indicates what information is needed to implement business judgment. Fig. 14 is a model of a conceptual framework leading to a decision.

It is possible to recognise three phases in the way a company may approach the question of international marketing. The three phases represent stages in a company's commitment to international marketing and the level of investment:

1. No-change phase;
2. production change;
3. capital-investment change.

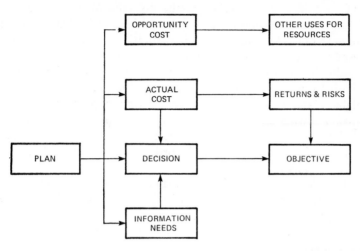

Fig. 14.—*Conceptual framework for decisions.*

In the first phase, no change is made in the company's organisation or production. Initially export business tends to originate in one of four ways outlined earlier in this chapter. The firm is unlikely to change its methods but will utilise surplus capacity to cope with export orders. The firm may, if it finds that export business is not disruptive to existing practice, extend its activities by looking for export opportunities in government publications, or specialist industry journals, such as *Contract Journal.*

Orders are accepted on a one-off basis and production is arranged as required, which may be temporary spare capacity, or by weekend or overtime working. If the latter method is used it will incur additional production costs as overtime working will be at a premium rate which can rarely be passed on in a higher price.

Most companies carrying on export business in this fashion are production-oriented, or at best, sales-oriented. This implies that the first consideration given to an order is whether it fits in with the company's existing production arrangements. Sales-orientation admits of the importance of the customer, but only as a means of satisfying production needs. In these organisations there is little marketing activity aimed at customer creation and satisfaction.

Companies which can see the benefits of regular export business usually progress to a more positive attitude. This leads them to actively seek export opportunities and to allocate some resources, office staff, warehouse and packing facilities and production to export business. This is the production-change phase in which some change in production generally takes place. Such change may recognise that export orders need special sewing machines, different standards of tools, special packing, different colour schemes. It may lead to the company setting aside some resources in order to accomplish the needs of the export market.

This level of commitment cannot be accomplished overnight. It may require changes in plant layout and personnel training; it may be necessary to appoint specialist staff such as a designer, or to send staff on courses for additional training or experience.

Adopting a continuing approach to exporting will need a formal search for export opportunities and their subsequent analysis. It will be necessary to appoint specialist marketing research staff to analyse the information, interpret it and communicate the results to the functional staff.

There is an increased level of expenditure in the production-change phases and therefore an increased risk. The level of investment need not be excessively high but even a limited amount increases the fixed costs and, since export markets are slow to develop, there can be some delay before the markets are sufficient to cover the increased fixed costs and begin to show a profit.

In the capital-investment phase of exporting the company will have become well established in export markets and the volume of business from overseas will be large and continuous. At this stage it will decide to invest in developing its international marketing activities. This may be by several means.

It may make substantial investments in plant modernisation and replacement to bring it up to the standards of its major competitors both at home and abroad. Increasing the size of the plant will permit economies of scale and this will be reflected in lower prices both at home and abroad, thereby creating more demand and eventually leading to a dominant position. It may decide to invest directly abroad in assembly or manufacturing capability. Revlon International, the American-based cosmetics giant, has invested heavily in virtually all overseas markets to some degree, according to the way the company views the prospects. In some countries fully-independent manufacturing companies have been created, such as their plant at Maesteg in South Wales; in others there exist different levels of involvement from packing and bottling plants to sales offices serviced from other factories.

Whichever way the firm decides, it is investing financial resources today with the expectation of receiving sufficient return in the future to repay the investment and make a worthwhile profit.

This date of anticipated recovery is important if the firm is to estimate its return with any accuracy. It will want to know at what date the revenue from the investment will exceed the cost of the investment, that is the pay-off date, as illustrated in Fig. 15.

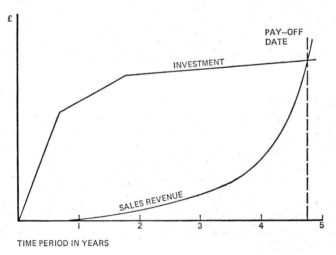

FIG. 15.—*Recovery of export investment.*

It is not sufficient to know only the pay-off date because that only implies the investment is recovered. The business purpose is profit and therefore even if the pay-off has been accomplished what is important to know is, how long the investment will be profitable. An investment which just manages to break-even has not been a success. From Fig. 15 it will be seen that initially the investment level is high but gradually falls off, while the sales revenue begins slowly but should eventually exceed the accumulated investment.

Investing large sums internationally, or on the basis of international business, requires a high level of skill and success depends upon assessment of long-term marketing objectives.

It does not always happen that a company progresses in this way. A company may stop at any one of the phases and they may be affected in different ways. An order which would require heavy investment or a production change in a small company may be dealt with in a no-change situation in a big company.

No-change decision-making

A company that secures an export order at a given price has several issues to decide. How much will it cost to produce the order and what will it cost to deliver? Is the margin between the cost of producing the order and the income derived from it sufficient to justify its acceptance? In a no-change situation we are only concerned with marginal variable costs since the fixed costs will normally be covered by sales in the domestic market.

Marginal costing
The evaluation of export orders in a no-change situation is best accomplished by a process of marginal costing which differentiates between fixed costs and variable costs. A company combines its resources with the aim of achieving a certain range of output. Within this normal range certain costs (machinery, plant, rates, etc.) are fixed while other costs vary according to output (labour, electricity, materials, etc.). Marginal costing is concerned with revealing what effects changes in output have on profitability.

Marginal cost is the addition to total cost resulting from the production of one more unit (or the savings in costs resulting from the production of one less). Table III shows the marginal cost of producing a man's two-piece suit. The difference between the marginal costs of the products manufactured and their selling prices is the contribution which each makes to total fixed costs and profits. In Table III the contribution is £2.40 per suit. The aggregate contribution of all products must in the long term cover the company's fixed costs and provide a satis-

business would have created problems. The capacity of the plant had reached its limits and the extra business would have caused overtime working, or sub-contracting, all of which would have resulted in an excessive marginal cost (*see* Fig. 16).

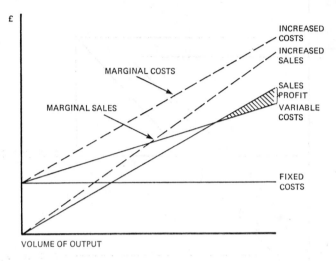

FIG. 16.—*Effect of increased exports on existing capacity.*

Production—change situation

If the export opportunities are beyond existing capacity but the company is confident of maintaining a sufficiently high volume of business it may opt for a production-change situation.

Supposing a company's costs and sales at full existing capacity are:

Sales per annum	£100,000
Variable costs	£60,000
Fixed costs	£20,000

It can achieve the extra output by overtime working, changes in plant layout or by means of work study and increased productivity. Any of these will result in a production change.

If the objective is to increase capacity by 25 per cent to deal with export demand, extra shifts may be introduced. This will increase the fixed costs but will permit an increase in capacity and should result in lower export prices. Fig. 17 illustrates the shift in the break-even point and the need for a sustained higher volume of business.

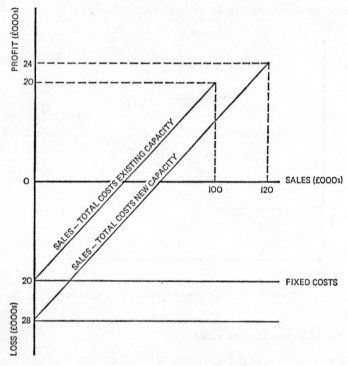

FIG. 17.—*Profit/volume graph.*

A production change of this nature should only be a short-term measure. It relies on the co-operation of workers who will have to work overtime, or some shift system, and it also risks capital since the machinery is being operated almost continuously. While this is fully utilising the machinery it does expose the firm in the event of breakdown. In the long term a firm that can sustain sales must look to a capital-investment change.

At this point the company has to decide whether to contract its selling activities abroad to stay within the existing capacity, or expand capacity. Both contain a strong element of risk. If the company limits its sales it is attempting to stand still. In a dynamic economic system this is not possible and so the firm falls behind competitors, who are able to expand and lower costs.

If the firm expands its capacity it must ensure a continuous flow of increased business or its fixed costs will be excessive. Two examples will illustrate this point.

In the early 1960s when Britain seemed poised to enter the European Economic Community, the Spencer Steel Works at Llanwern was built with a production capacity designed for an enlarged European home market. After Britain failed to achieve membership the steel works had to operate at half capacity with disastrous results for profitability.

Also in the 1960s many companies saw potential for consumer goods in the Soviet Union. A shoe manufacturer, after trying for years, was finally awarded a huge order. To fulfil the order, and anticipating more to follow, he expanded his plant considerably but no more orders came and he eventually went out of business.

Capital-investment situation

A major change in output necessitates a recombination of resources. It is rarely possible to expand output and achieve benefits of scale without incurring increasing fixed costs which make low levels of output more costly. Therefore a company embarking upon a capital investment programme to deal with anticipated increases in export turnover must ensure the volume materialises. Fig. 18 illustrates how costs increase either side of the optimum level and suggests that a careful analysis of potential overseas demand is necessary to ensure the anticipated return is attained by the pay-off date.

Because of the delay in recovering the investment the changing value of money over a period of time has to be accounted for, and *discounting* techniques employed. It is important to understand that £1 today is worth more than £1 at some future date. This is not solely the result of inflation, but also because the £1 received today could be used to earn in the intervening time, and this is known as the *time value of money concept.*

The rate of return on capital is defined as the ratio of profit to capital. The profit is usually expressed as an average over the life of the project and the capital is the original outlay. The following calculation illustrates the concept by comparing two alternative projects assuming one represents an overseas investment.

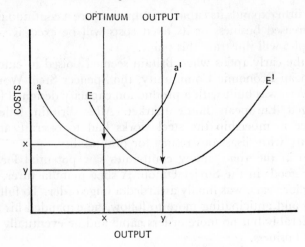

FIG. 18.—*Changes in production level.*
a–a′ : Existing production.
E–E′ : Proposed capital-investment change.

Project	Investment £	Net profit (£000) Years 1	2	3	4	5	6
A	25,000	4	5	6	7	5	2
B	35,000	5	8	9	10	7	4

This can now be calculated as follows to show average profits:

$$A = \frac{£4 + 5 + 6 + 7 + 5 + 2}{6} = \frac{£29}{6} = £4,830$$

$$B = \frac{£5 + 8 + 9 + 10 + 7 + 4}{6} = \frac{£43}{6} = £7,160$$

$$\text{Rate of return} = A = \frac{4,830}{25,000} \times 100 = 19.3\%$$

$$B = \frac{7,160}{35,000} \times 100 = 20.4\%$$

In this example project B would be chosen in preference to A. While the rate of return method takes into account all earnings it does not reflect the true value of near profits as opposed to distant ones. The major weakness is the missing consideration of compound interest which the money might be expected to earn between the date of investment and the date of receipt.

One hundred pounds invested now at 10 per cent will produce in one year—100 + (100 × 10%) = £110. In two years' time the investment will be worth 110 + (110 × 10%) = £121.

Discounting is the opposite of compounding and is used to determine the present value of future cash flows. Discounting tables are calculated by the formula:

$$\frac{1}{(1+i)n}$$

When a project's discounted cash flow has been calculated it is compared with other factors to decide whether it is financially acceptable; these are (a) the firm's cost of capital, and (b) returns on alternative projects.

The minimum return that is acceptable on any project is the rate of interest which the company has to pay on the capital invested. Since a company might draw capital from different sources at different costs problems can arise. It should aim at a financial structure which minimises the weighted average costs of the different sources of capital.

Applying these techniques to the problem of whether or not to invest internationally the company would be especially concerned to assess the demand for the products in the overseas markets. It would want to know, in addition to levels of demand, estimates of market size, the market share that they should aim for, growth rates in various segments of the markets and levels of competitive activity. It will be concerned to know that the determined method of output will provide the capacity for expansion and also that adequate maintenance and servicing is available. It will want to assess likely production and marketing costs including fixed and variable costs. Finally it will want to estimate the effects of any taxation which is going to arise at home and abroad, such as corporation tax, allowances and investments grants.

It is almost impossible to predict every eventuality in the marketing environment, especially internationally. In 1975 there was a *coup d'état* in Nigeria, long regarded as the most stable state in Africa. How the change of government affected investments was not clear and future investors had to pause to see what would happen.

The capital-investment situation is a risk strategy and ideally a company looks at the "best" likely result and the "worst" likely result. Before embarking upon a strategy abroad the company should have gained experience of exporting and have the human resources available to understand international marketing problems.

The multinational strategy

Business is going global as the search for profits pushes more firms into the world. Many companies have operated internationally for many years. Shell, Unilever, General Foods, Standard Oil and Revlon International have virtually no home markets. Many firms, particularly in the United States, have been obliged to invest abroad due to dwindling returns on investment figures at home. Some years ago DuPont closed plants in the United States and opened in Europe where its return was a percentage higher, but of the multi-millions involved, one per cent is a big consideration on corporate profits.

Multinational companies are becoming features of world trade—firms like Ford that can switch production from one country to another according to returns, labour relations and economic conditions. A multinational company is one that meets two basic tests. It has a manufacturing base in at least one foreign country, and having a genuine international perspective its management makes decisions on production, research and marketing in terms of alternatives available anywhere in the world.

There has been developing during the last fifteen years new approaches aimed at minimising the risks involved in moving internationally. In concept the aim is to extend the role of planning to the broadest possible scale by understanding the ultimate goal of the corporation. This can be summarised in the term "global planning."

This concept has a number of characteristics. First, it assumes that the company in making a first move has as its goal establishing a base which will not at a later date inhibit further expansion as a second goal. If it moves to a country where it identifies a certain level of present activity and potential but later finds this to be of limited potential, or there are legal restrictions on the way the company can perform, it may find it has placed itself in a "strait-jacket" and can neither expand or get out, except at an unacceptable cost.

The second goal implies a willingness on the part of the corporation to expand its overseas operation in terms of where in the world it should invest its resources to provide the best long-term use of them.

The first stage in this way of thinking forward is for the company to appoint a committee with the objective of formulating the company's international plans on a basis of world-wide policies. It must be able to make decisions on a range of topics:

1. Ensure the total company structure is aware of the overall objective and the ultimate goal.

2. Determine which countries should be selected for initial expansion; this must depend upon the kind of output the firm is engaged in but unless it is raw materials of some kind, this will usually mean concentrating on the developed countries with high levels of demand and spending power.

3. Organise the world markets on some acceptable basis of segmentation; again this will depend upon products, markets and objectives.

4. Identify the key markets, generally Europe or the United States, as representing the highest percentage of the free world markets and aim to identify existing opportunities and ways of exploiting them.

5. Freeze existing international arrangements of licensing and distribution until an overall concept has been created.

6. Investigate existing practices among present international operators, and be prepared to learn from their experience and mistakes.

At the outset the company must examine its existing selling and licensing arrangements to see whether they preclude alteration or development. This is a complex area which companies should make themselves aware of as there is now in existence a great deal of agency and licensing legislation developed to protect nationals in their own countries and which in the main is not helpful to companies having to make arrangements.

Potential markets will be determined as a result of secondary research into existing information and from reports of governments, trade associations and other sources which might be available to the company. This market research must be linked to product evaluation to identify key factors that will permit development as quickly as possible.

In the second phase executives will visit the countries initially

c

selected to investigate on the ground any areas of doubt. They can also review the economic and political background for markets as a whole and particular aspects or areas. This is then developed to produce a precise account of the specific markets selected. This must lead to an analysis of the company's strengths and weaknesses and comparison made with those of the major competitors.

In the third phase of the process an operational strategy for the long term is devised to enable the company to capitalise on the information revealed in its research stage. It will also seek to identify any interactions between markets arising from economic links.

The final stage is the development of a marketing plan based on the operational strategy and enabling a definition of the organisational needs. It is also necessary to create a statutory organisation that will provide ownership links with the parent company and satisfy the needs of the local national laws.

Once the company is established in the overseas market it becomes important to determine how co-operation between the new company and the parent company is to take place. It will need procedures laid down for organisational development, management style and co-operation, control systems, communications and a method of evaluating any new investment proposals.

There are a number of advantages to this kind of global approach to total corporate planning. It means that it is possible to set long-term objectives and develop a long-term strategy before the actual establishment abroad, thus avoiding conflict later. By investigating a number of countries at the outset, the selection basis is broad enough to allow a wide comparison of markets and the resultant storage of data permits integration between markets at a later date. This in turn enables multi-country decisions to be taken as shifts in cash flows alter the relationships between markets.

All the factors just mentioned depend upon understanding the cost structures of the various alternatives and in this the multinational company is no different, but only more complex than the national company embarking upon international marketing. The underlying need remains the ability to assess markets less by rule of thumb, hunch and experience and more by a positive science-based system of analyses.

CHAPTER FOUR

Operational research in marketing

Introduction

Most books on operational research, hereafter referred to as O.R., put important emphasis on techniques for the solution of problems. In this treatment of the subject, in its use to marketing, it is intended to aid understanding of the nature of O.R. methods, encourage a critical attitude to models and examine the methods by which the parameters are determined.

In Chapter 2 the problems of decision-making were discussed and the difficulties involved in decision-making in a state of uncertainty were considered. Many decisions in industry are difficult and indeed everyday decisions by individuals are often arrived at by the purely subjective analysis, frequently based on inaccurate information: for example, a businessman employed four teams of O.R. men until he found the one which agreed with his preconceived solution.

O.R. introduces an objective analysis of alternative solutions and therefore provides a more accurate basis for decision-making. O.R. introduces quantitative concepts to marketing decisions which are becoming increasingly important in an area of business not generally known for numeracy in its problem-solving. It must be stressed that what is important to marketing management is to understand the mechanics of problem-solving and methods of constructing the framework for analysis rather than being able to do the actual calculating, which can be handled by computers.

O.R. is useful when the problem facing management is complex enough to suggest a number of alternative factors which have to be balanced against one another. Frequently there are a number of chance factors which influence the circumstances of the problems. O.R. is an aid to solving problems when the scale of operations is so large that the likely return from a study is high enough to justify the cost of research.

A favoured area for applying O.R. has been in devising routeing schemes for transport vehicles. In 1967 Cadburys wished to overhaul its existing system of vehicles and depots by which they distribute from factories to retailers. O.R. was used to investigate methods of improving vehicle routeing. For a month, comparisons were made between the existing routeing system's "best" solution and the computer output based on sophisticated mathematical equations. The results indicated that savings were possible but those were offset by the high cost of data processing. It was also found that the computer methods would be impossible to implement. A simple manual method was developed aimed at minimising the numbers of vehicles in use. This showed higher savings than the best devised by the computer, without the cost of data processing and the difficulties of implementation.

O.R. was developed from the needs of wartime planning and problem-solving. The discipline was developed essentially through the work of Professor Blackett who had been given the task of making the best use of the new Radar system. This he agreed to do providing he could select his own team and, on the agreement of the Ministry of Defence, he chose three psychologists, two mathematical physicists, two mathematicians, an astrophysicist, a surveyor, a general physicist and an army officer.

This team was selected partially because of the shortage of scientists and partially for the diversity of their skills and intellectual approach. "Blackett's Circus," as the team became known, was very successful and continued to tackle a variety of complex problems throughout the war. Blackett's team developed a distinctive approach which proved applicable to complex problems derived from the operations of complex organisations. His work had three distinctive characteristics:

1. The systems approach

When faced with a difficult problem it is natural for most people to divide it into manageable parts and attempt to examine each part in isolation. Essentially O.R. is a systems approach and derives its success from a process of expanding the problem instead of dividing it.

In marketing the problems are interacting ones, since a solution here is likely to have an effect there. The environment is itself highly complex with many legal, economic, technological and human constraints. In circumstances where all parts of the system interact, it is essential that parts are not isolated, but the significant interactions are identified and the combined impact on the total organisation is measured. The inter-disciplinary approach was stressed in Chapter 1 in relation to specific marketing problems of advertising, pricing, product evaluation and environmental studies.

Solutions to O.R. problems have an effect upon company policy, as indicated by the following quote from *O.R. Comes of Age: A Review of the Work of the Operational Research of the National Coal Board 1948–1969*:

"In general, O.R. is rarely concerned with individual operations in detail, and only the overall characteristics of these operations will enter into its models of wider spheres of company activity. The viewpoint could be summarised as implying that workshop efficiency is all very well, but that the O.R. scientist aspired to influence Board policy."

Solutions to O.R. problems have an effect upon company policy; it is, however, not always possible to produce solutions within the constraints of company policy. The work of O.R. staff is to solve complex marketing problems and give the answer to management, and it is management's task to decide on the form of their implementation and their effect upon policy.

A London department store was alarmed at falling profits and began a process of recording and analysing the performance of each department to discover where the losses were originating. It was found that all the departments, except the restaurant, were incurring a loss. On that basis, only the restaurant would have been retained, but clearly that could not be the solution. It is only when the whole system is examined and not the various parts in isolation that a satisfactory solution is obtained.

2. Inter-disciplinary approach

Blackett's original team was inter-disciplinary largely because of the extreme pressures of wartime upon the availability of scientists. It resulted in an original approach that had breadth of vision and was highly successful. Business problems have become increasingly complex and rarely can a single discipline produce the best solution.

Consumer behaviour derives its understanding of marketing factors from the specialist work of sociologists, anthropologists, psychologists, advertising people and economists. To their results can be applied the work of statisticians and mathematicians. Since we use the work of these varied scientists to create original concepts it seems natural to use them to produce solutions to original problems.

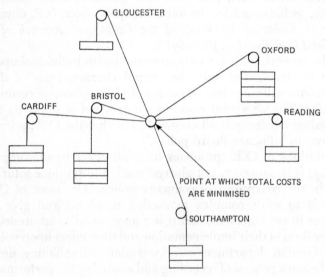

FIG. 19.—*Weighted location model.*

Advertising and sales promotion are a part of the total communications system in marketing, along with the sales and public relations. It is a vastly complicated area involving as it does, visual and design problems, motivation problems, psychology of learning and perception, social problems of class and attitudes, communications problems which can include radio, cinema, television and their attendant production and technological processes, product design and engineering.

Physical distribution is another area of great complexity, ranging from stock control problems of a statistical nature to legal restrictions on the size of vehicles and how long a man may drive in a working day.

In spite of the inter-disciplinary nature of the problems most firms expect one man, probably the marketing manager, and perhaps his staff, to find adequate solutions.

Give the sales manager the job of solving a stock control problem and he will probably decide the solution is to carry sufficient stock to meet all his requirements at any time. The production controller is more concerned with long production runs and so long as the stock control problem does not interfere with that he is satisfied. The accountant will be anxious about the amount of money tied up in stock. The solution to problems like these lies somewhere between all the single answers and an inter-disciplinary approach is the only way of getting a viable solution.

3. Scientific method

The third and most important characteristic of O.R. is its scientific approach. It aims to reproduce a problem in some model form which can then be manipulated and analysed to discover the "best" solution. A marketing manager can build a model that will simulate his operational situation and by manipulation it can either provide a solution to his marketing problem or be used to predict the future. A simple example will demonstrate the O.R. approach.

A typical problem to be found in marketing is the location of a warehouse, or distribution centre. Fig. 19 is a weighted location model illustrating a simplified location problem.

There are six cities to be served by a central distribution point. The level of demand varies and the problem is to locate the distribution centre at a point from which the total transport will be at a minimum.

To *indicate* a solution to the problem, a vertical map is produced with a friction-free pulley screwed into the map at each of the locations. Threads are put over the wheels and are attached to weights representing the various relative levels of demand. For instance, if demand at Bristol is twice that of Reading then it will carry double the weight. The six threads are connected to a single ring and the system allowed to find its own stability. Where the ring settles will be the point at which the total costs are at a minimum (the point at which all the forces balance). It can be quickly adapted to take in more localities. If transport costs are higher on one route than another this can be incorporated by increasing the weights.

A model such as this gives an approximation to the truth; it has many limitations, among them different standards of road, degrees of congestion and frequency of delivery.

Operational research method

The Operational Research Society officially defines the O.R. method as:

"The attack of modern science on complex problems arising in the direction and management of large systems of men, machines and money in industry, business, government and defence. The distinctive approach is to develop a scientific model of the system, incorporating measurement of factors such as chance and risk, in order to predict and compare the outcomes of alternative decisions, strategies and controls. The purpose is to help management determine its policy and actions scientifically."

Fig. 20 illustrates the O.R. method. Recognition of the problem demands an objective outlook which people involved in the day-to-day activities can rarely bring to bear. An O.R. team is usually sufficiently removed to recognise that what management defines as a problem is often only a symptom.

In defining the problem an attempt is made to state in precise terms the various interacting variables and to identify the independent ones. An example is the firm faced with steep rises in the cost of invoices. An examination of printing costs revealed nothing that would account for the high costs. It was only when an examination was made of the use to which they were put that the real problem became clearer. The amount of detail on the invoices varied a great deal so that while some were filled to capacity, others were nearly empty. An analysis of past invoices was made and as a result the size of the forms was reduced. The final size was decided after experiments with different forms to minimise wastage.

In constructing a model of the problem situation we do not have to involve ourselves with higher mathematics as a necessity. The weighted location model is an example of construction

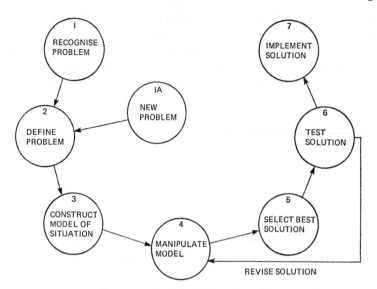

FIG. 20.—*Operational research method.*

in which the minimum of mathematical skill is needed. In practical terms there is a range of modelling tools from which the technique can be selected which is most suited to the task.

Mathematical models can be used where the variables can be precisely defined. Production problems and transport problems, where exact details can be known, can therefore be tackled mathematically.

Sometimes a problem involves variables which cannot be defined accurately and a solution can only be found by a process of trial and error. In these circumstances mathematical models cannot be used. Some time ago the author was involved in finding a solution to a problem arising from the operation of a mobile library service for a County Council. The library was a van servicing some twenty villages. The van called at each village in a cycle but this should have varied according to the population and the number of readers, which in turn varied according to the time of year, weather and amount of rural work. How many vans were needed and in what order should a van call at a village and with what frequency? The variables were seemingly endless. The method chosen was linear programming for a transportation problem, but it must be admitted that while suggestions were made it was a situation in which a complete solution was not possible.

There are also marketing problems in which variables are not controllable—customers calling at a store is an example. Traffic counts on numbers passing key points in a shopping area will do no more than provide guidance and a strict mathematical analysis is impossible.

There are common forms of model in which the marketing manager may be presented with a schematic flow diagram. Such a diagram sets out the range of factors affecting supply and demand. The illustration in Fig. 21 is concerned with the question of appliance replacement. It may be said that it is concerned with defining all the factors needed to be understood and measured to interpret the complete situation in quantifiable terms. Such a model has its limitations and may not even be computable, but it is an essential aid in understanding the market structure and also the information flows for decision-making. O.R. is essentially a technique involving logic rather than mathematics.

In selecting the best solution we are concerned with optimising the variables which might mean the most profitable, least costly, shortest distance, frequency of calls, or some other goal.

A solution must be tested operationally since laboratory

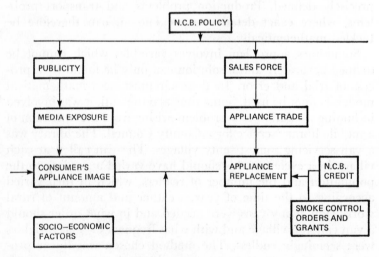

FIG. 21.—*Schematic model dealing with appliance replacement.*

conditions rarely perform in the operational role. A company developed a strong concrete adhesive which was subjected to all the usual tests in the laboratory, before being tried in the market. It comprised two tins, the adhesive and a catalyst. In the laboratory it worked perfectly, while under operational conditions the mixture "went-off" so quickly the brush stuck to the wall!

Many marketing problems work in theory or under test but they are not so successful in practice. When faults are found in the testing stage, they can be revised if necessary without doing too much damage.

"As a field for O.R. investigations, marketing may be considered as one step more difficult than the problems of colliery operations . . ."

O.R. Comes of Age, edited by Rolfe C. Tomlinson,
Tavistock Publications, 1971.

Implementing the work of O.R. within an organisation can bring troubles, particularly if the personnel involved have not been fully informed of the purpose of the change.

Generally it is better to introduce change quickly and get it over with so that people's resistance is not allowed time to develop. It is not only operatives and salesmen who resist change, very often the greatest resistance is found in middle management and even among senior management who might have initiated the original investigation but do not like the solution.

O.R. is concerned with decision-making in management situations which are both complex and uncertain. To tackle a problem with any chance of success the main decision-making points must be recognised and then used to identify the points at which the decisions are most sensitive. A marketing executive who spends £10 million a year in conditions in which the results will be roughly the same however he allocates expenditure, will be less sensitive than a man spending £1 million in a critical situation in which his actions can create disaster if wrong.

A second criterion relating to these decision-making points is the availability of data. Ideally an O.R. team select problems in which there is quantitative data available rather than qualitative data which is difficult to rationalise and treat with logic.

Operations research techniques

O.R. is a method of making decisions and not simply a collection of tools from which the team select the appropriate one. When management is faced with recurring decisions it can employ a technique which has been successful in similar circumstances.

Linear programming is the task of allocating a limited resource to alternative demands in an effective way. The technique has many varied applications, diverse in their setting and methods of solution. It can be used to suggest solutions to problems of the lowest cost programme for distribution, determining the most economical mix of factors to meet product specifications or determining the most economic allocation of available capital to different uses.

The techniques of linear programming are of two different kinds, transportation problems and blending problems.

Example of transportation problem

Distribution is an example of a transportation problem. A large animal-feedstuffs group has five major marketing outlets in Shrewsbury, York, Durham, Salisbury and Exeter. These are supplied by three units at Cardiff, Norwich and Bristol, each of which has a limitation in its capacity determining availability of the product. In each area market demand determines quantities to be produced. The problem is to allocate the production at the three mills to the five sales outlets to meet demand and minimise transport costs.

The capacity of the three mills is Cardiff (X) 20,000; Norwich (Y) 30,000 and Bristol (Z) 24,000 units. The sales distribution outlets' demands are Shrewsbury (A) 10,000; York (B) 12,000; Durham (C) 8,000; Salisbury (D) 18,000 and Exeter (E) 26,000 units. The cost of transporting each unit is stated in Table VIII.

Having outlined the problem the next step is to construct a model of the situation which in this case is a matrix, Table VIII. This matrix illustrates the conditions and by manipulating it an optimum solution can be determined.

To manipulate the model to get an answer, an initial solution is first suggested. This is done by assigning the various units of

TABLE VIII. *Transportation costs.*

From mills	A Shrewsbury	B York	C Durham	D Salisbury	E Exeter	(000s) Total
X Cardiff	32	32	34	30	34	20
Y Norwich	24	32	30	36	38	30
Z Bristol	36	34	32	38	36	24
Total (000s)	10	12	8	18	26	74

production in an arbitrary way that ignores transportation costs. This begins in the top left-hand corner, and all the units are assigned as in Table IX. The total transport cost on this initial basis is now calculated, which in this case gives a value of 2,524 as in Table X.

TABLE IX. *Initial solution.*

	A	B	C	D	E	(000s) Total
X	10 32	8 32	34	30	2 34	20
Y	24	4 32	8 30	18 36	38	30
Z	36	34	32	38	24 36	24
Total (000s)	10	12	8	18	26	74

TABLE X. *Total transportation cost—initial solution.*

X–A	10 × 32 =	320
X–B	8 × 32 =	256
Y–B	4 × 32 =	128
Y–C	8 × 30 =	240
Y–D	18 × 36 =	648
X–E	2 × 34 =	68
Z–E	24 × 36 =	864
	Total	2,524

The model is again manipulated to see whether a better

solution is possible. Each square is examined and assignments are shifted where possible to see if reduced costs can result. It is important to see that the conditions of units available and units required remain the same. Table XI is the best solution and the total transport cost calculated in Table XII to give a value of 2,336.

TABLE XI. *Best solution.*

	A	B	C	D	E	(000s) Total
X	^{32}	^{32}	^{36}	18 ^{30}	2 ^{34}	20
Y	10 ^{24}	12 ^{32}	8 ^{30}	^{36}	^{38}	30
Z	^{36}	^{34}	^{32}	^{38}	24 ^{36}	24
Total (000s)	10	12	8	18	26	74

TABLE XII. *Total transportation costs—best solution.*

Y–A	$10 \times 24 =$	240
Y–B	$12 \times 32 =$	384
Y–C	$8 \times 30 =$	240
X–D	$18 \times 30 =$	540
X–E	$2 \times 34 =$	68
Z–E	$24 \times 36 =$	864
	Total	2,336

The method employed of trial and error establishes an arrangement for the product's distribution in such a way as will minimise transport costs.

Once the satisfactory solution to the problem has been arrived at it remains to be tested and if the findings are confirmed, implemented into general practice. The implementation will encounter the associated problems of communication, resistance to change and the problems of inter-personal relationships. Introduction will be eased by a knowledge of the behavioural sciences.

A similar linear programming approach can be used in the following example. Two breweries, A and B, are in competition in the West Country. Both breweries, being small local companies, rely on brand loyalty in the face of national competition, and aim their policy to appeal to different segments of the population.

In the past both breweries have almost equally shared the markets of the surrounding area, and now the marketing director of brewery B has decided to quantify his decision-making processes so as to attempt to gain a larger share of the market in terms of the potential volume.

The marketing director lists the alternatives available to him, as well as the likely, and possible responses available to his competitor, brewery A.

Alternative strategies available to brewery B:

1. Buy beer from a national brewery and resell at regular price.
2. Brew homemade beer and sell at reduced price.
3. Buy beer from national brewery and sell at reduced price.

In response to these strategies it is believed that brewery A can adopt one of the following:

1. Brew homemade beer and sell at regular price.
2. Buy beer from national brewery and sell at reduced price.
3. Buy beer from national brewery and sell at regular price.
4. Brew top quality beer and sell at high price.

Assuming the likely response by brewery A, the marketing director of brewery B is able to calculate the percentage gain or loss in market share by his company as represented in the matrix as follows:

		brewery A		
brewery B	A1	A2	A3	A4
B1	−5%	2%	0%	7%
B2	5%	6%	4%	8%
B3	4%	0%	2%	−3%

From analysis of the figures the marketing director can pose two questions: What is the optimal strategy for his brewery to pursue? What will be the net change in the long term?

His reading of the matrix will be on the basis that his competitor will counter his strategy with the one that permits brewery B to gain the least share of the market. Thus if he takes B1, his competitor will not follow A4, since this will allow B to gain 7 per cent of the market. Brewery A's response will be the one that puts the greatest defensive pressure on brewery B.

In this instance the marketing director will follow strategy B2 which it is anticipated will provoke response A3 from his competitor. The net change in the long term will be that brewery B will gain 4 per cent of the market at brewery A's expense.

Example of blending problem
The blending techniques of linear programming are more general in their range of application than the transportation techniques. The technique involves constructing a graphical presentation (a model) upon which are plotted the various constraints and objectives.

To give an example of the O.R. method applied to blending techniques let us consider a product-mix problem.

A factory has one production line of hairdryers and one of electric fans. The main manufacturing departments are: machine shop, moulding department, motor assembly, hair-dryer assembly and fan assembly. The problem is one of allocating resources between the production and marketing of hairdryers and electric fans.

The capacities of the departments are:

Department	Hairdryers		Electric fans
Machine shop	15,000	or	12,000
Moulding dept.	10,000	or	18,000
Motor assembly	12,000	or	14,000
Hairdryer assembly	8,000		
Electric fan assembly			10,000

The first three departments produce both hairdryers and electric fans in the proportion described above, *i.e.* moulding department could produce 10,000 hairdryers or 18,000 fans. The other two assembly departments are specialised and separate.

The profit is £5 per hairdryer, and £6 per electric fan. Marketing and production management's problem is how many of each product should be produced to maximise profits.

In constructing a model the various limitations which must be shown in the graph (*see* Fig. 22) are as follows:

1. Assembly   Hairdryers, 8,000; electric fans, 10,000.
2. Machine shop   The factory can produce 15,000 hairdryers and no fans, or 12,000 fans and no hairdryers.
3. Moulding dept.   The factory can produce 10,000 hairdryers and no fans, or 18,000 fans and no hairdryers.
4. Motor assembly   The factory can produce 12,000 hairdryers and no fans, or 14,000 fans and no hairdryers.

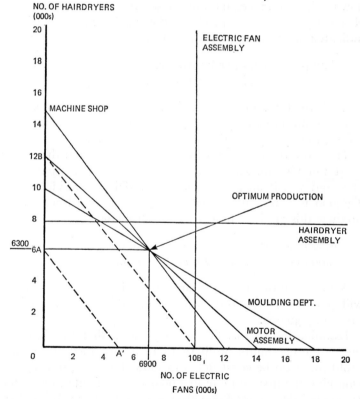

Fig. 22.—*Blending graph.*
A–A′ : Profit line for £30,000.
B–B′ : Profit line for £60,000.

These figures are now plotted on a graph and lines drawn to represent the limits beyond which the factory cannot produce. The factory cannot produce 8,000 hairdryers and 12,000 fans as no department could handle the volume. It could make 6,000 hairdryers and 6,000 fans which is within the capacity of all departments. The machine shop is capable of producing 10,000 hairdryers and 2,000 fans but this is outside the capacity of the moulding department and therefore the factory as a whole. The term "linear programming" is derived from the use of straight lines to express all the relationships on the graph.

Manipulating the model

Once the model has been constructed the O.R. worker can now use it to produce an optimum solution in which the output of hairdryers and fans produces the maximum profit. This is indicated on the graph by a profit line.

The profit is £5 per hairdryer,
£6 per electric fan.

If x is the total number of hairdryers produced, then $x \times £5$ = the profit on hairdryers; if y is the total of electric fans produced, then $y \times £6$ = the profit on electric fans.

Therefore the total profit would be $5x + 6y$ and this should be at a maximum. The graph can be used to show what values of x and y will maximise the profit. If it is considered that £30,000 is a reasonable profit how many hairdryers would produce this profit or how many electric fans?

6,000 hairdryers at £5 each = £30,000; or
5,000 electric fans at £6 each = £30,000.

A line is drawn on the graph through the two points that will give this profit and anywhere along this line will provide a profit of £30,000.

Examination of this line clearly shows that this is by no means the maximum profit that can be obtained and further profit lines can be constructed to show different profit figures. Doubling the first estimate to £60,000 would entail producing 12,000 hairdryers or 10,000 electric fans but this is beyond the capacity of the motor assembly department. It is necessary to find the profit line that just permits a feasible production according to the limitations of production but which is furthest from the point of origin, and the points at which this line touches the outside limits of the graph will show what quantities can be produced.

In the example the optimum production is:

6,300 hairdryers at £5 each   = £31,500
6,900 electric fans at £6 each = £41,400
_____
Total profit   = £72,900

Blending techniques are very flexible and can be used to quickly take into account changes in circumstances such as shortages restricting the output of any single department, or new methods of production permitting an increased profit for a product. However, beyond three products blending cannot be used and computer techniques have to be employed. Computers have made it possible to make calculations which could not have been previously attempted.

A first attempt to use linear programming by the National Coal Board when calculating machines were all that was available meant lengthy delays in producing results. One involving 135 sources of supply and forty-five customers took a week. Attempts were made to solve a problem involving 600 sources of supply and 150 demand points, but these were apparently unsuccessful, but a computer took only seconds to solve a problem involving 2,500 points of supply and 150 demand points, although collection and processing of the data took weeks.

Critical path analysis

Companies concerned with the increasing cost and time of processing new products, from their concept and subsequent research until production is initiated, have undertaken studies known by the term Critical Path Analysis (C.P.A.).

The main purpose of C.P.A. is in analysing and providing surveillance for novel programmes for which no standard times, costs and data are available. It is applicable to a wide range of marketing activities and programmes, including new product innovation, advertising campaigns, distribution problems, marketing research programmes and new market exploitation.

All are problems involving situations in which control has to evolve as the programme is unfolded.

The fundamental aim of the C.P.A. is to determine the longest time path of activities that are required to terminate a project. Once the critical path time needed to complete a project is known, management is able to allocate to each activity a time schedule permitting the substitution of sub-critical activities that need capital and manpower and so minimise the total cost of the project.

First the planning group establishes the programme network. In any project there will be some activities that must precede others, some will be dependent upon the completion of earlier stages, and a number may be done concurrently.

Fig. 23 is an arrow diagram which indicates the critical path in a typical new product development programme. The event code determines the activities as follows:

> *Event*
> A   Market research for new product.
> B   Development of prototype.
> C   Market feasibility study.
> D   Initial advertising campaign planning.
> E   Introductory campaign layout.
> F   Initial production batch.
> G   Prototype laboratory testing completed.
> H   Field test of prototype.
> I   Evaluation of field test.
> J   Financial aspects analysed.
> K   Development of bulk production methods.
> L   Quality control feasibility report.
> M   Final production model approved.
> N   Introductory advertising approved.
> O   Distribution channels decisions confirmed.
> P   Go or no-go decision.

The code also determines their sequence in completing the programme and is represented on the arrow diagram (Fig. 23) by the letters A–P. The sequence of the events is shown by arrows, indicating which are dependent upon completion of an earlier stage. Once the directed network diagram is established the planning group can proceed to the second stage.

The number on each arrow indicates the next steps to be

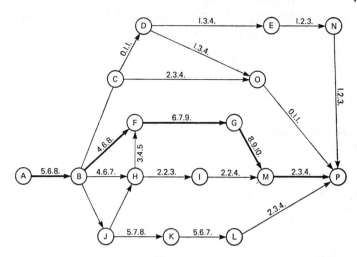

FIG. 23.—*Arrow diagram.*

taken. The department responsible for the activity has to estimate times. It will estimate the most optimistic time in which
its activity could be completed, the pessimistic estimate for
completion and the normal, or most likely time. The planner
compiles a list such as the following, which is arranged to an
expected time and extended to a cumulative expected time for
the overall project.

Event	Expected average time	Cumulative expected time in months
A	0	0
B	5.6.8./3 = 6·3	6·3
F	4.6.8./3 = 6·0	12·3
G	6.7.9./3 = 7·3	19·6
M	2.3.4./3 = 3·0	22·6
P	2.3.4./3 = 3·0	25·6

In the example the path from event D, introductory advertising campaign layout, shows the fastest time as 1 month,
worst time as 4 months and most likely time as 3 months,
giving an average expected time of 2·6 months. When this
calculation has been completed for each event a final figure for
the total time becomes available.

Each chain of events from beginning to end is examined in
turn and the one that takes the longest is the critical path—in the

example, ABFGMP, the list above, which shows a time of 25·6 months and is the expected time of completion for the project.

Critical path analysis offers a substantial benefit in defining future events and indicating how long they will take and enabling resources to be handled more efficiently. In the example arrow diagram, Fig. 23, no advertising expenditure need be incurred until all preceding events have been implemented.

By employing three estimates for performance the method indicates where the greatest uncertainties lie and where special attention is needed to ensure that no avoidable hold-up is permitted. In the example the greatest difference lies between events B and F where the difference between best and worst is four months. Management will want to know why this uncertainty exists and if possible remove its cause.

There is an important element of motivation embodied here. Each department knows what responsibility it has for the final completion and how its part fits the total project. It provides identifiable objectives for management at all levels.

All the activities in the network can be subjected to cost analysis. Resources which are employed in a sub-critical path can, if necessary, be re-allocated to hasten the critical path. It is an important technique for marketing both in identifying future events and providing surveillance and control.

Operations research provides a systematic approach to problem solving in all areas but it is particularly useful in a situation of such uncertainty. Sound marketing strategy depends upon knowledge, especially when decisions based on uncertainty have far-reaching effects on the company's policy and future. O.R. is very much dependent upon the continual support of marketing research to provide data which will permit opportunity maximisation policies to be implemented.

CHAPTER FIVE

Marketing models

The use of marketing models

In Chapter 4, "Operational research," we looked at techniques of providing for decisions in conditions of uncertainty and lack of data. The use of arrow diagrams, transportation and blending techniques involves the creation of models to describe situations and by manipulation of these produce solutions which can then be tested.

Management science makes great use of models and they are one of the central defining concepts in the discipline. P. Kotler defines a model in the following manner:

"The choice of a set of variables and a specification of their interrelationships designed to represent some real system or process, in whole or in part."
Marketing Management, Analysis, Planning and Control,
Prentice-Hall, 1967.

Model building to describe situations in business has derived from the work of operational research. They can be fairly simple statements of a particular market situation in which the main purpose is to focus executive attention on specific problems and create a circumstance in which a logical statement of the situation has to be made. They can also be an advanced mathematical statement of a situation and its attendant variables that has to be implemented and manipulated by a computer. Either way marketing models are intended to aid management in understanding an existing situation or predicting a future event.

On the whole model building in marketing is not widespread although the increased competitiveness of the last few years has

77

encouraged its greater use. The current economic problems of declining markets, of falling consumer spending power and an extreme deficit on the balance of payments represents a situation in which the use of models could be very helpful to management in cutting costs, replacing markets and understanding its future strategy, but unfortunately model building can be expensive and in situations of persistent losses, or at best falling profits, firms are reluctant to spend in this area.

Many marketing managers who are involved in the practical day-to-day running of businesses feel that marketing is concerned with creative flair and business intuition. They are resistant to scientific analysis based on hypotheses. In today's increasingly difficult conditions there is scope for both.

Creating a model

The creation of models varies according to their complexity. Some appear deceptively easy in their construction but the interrelationships are important and it is at this stage of thinking through the model that much of its subsequent value is determined.

Whether drawn or mathematical, a model is a formal statement of a situation and its variables but models also exist in a much less formal state. An experienced salesman who intends calling on a new client develops an implicit model in his head. This mental model has a core which is a descriptive model of the buyer's problem and the means by which the salesman's products or services can provide a solution. The model will also include his moves in response to the buyer's reactions and leads to a final decision model determining moves and counters. This is shown in Fig. 24, although the detail in the salesman's head is not going to be arranged so logically, although if asked to commit them to paper he would probably write down most of the items.

A refinement of the mental model occurs when the executive commits ideas to paper in the form of a marketing plan. The marketing plan is an explicit model illustrating how resources will be allocated to meet specific objectives.

Fig. 25 illustrates the complexity of a model based on a marketing plan. Such a model is a blueprint of a complete market structure. Each of the boxes in turn becomes a model of

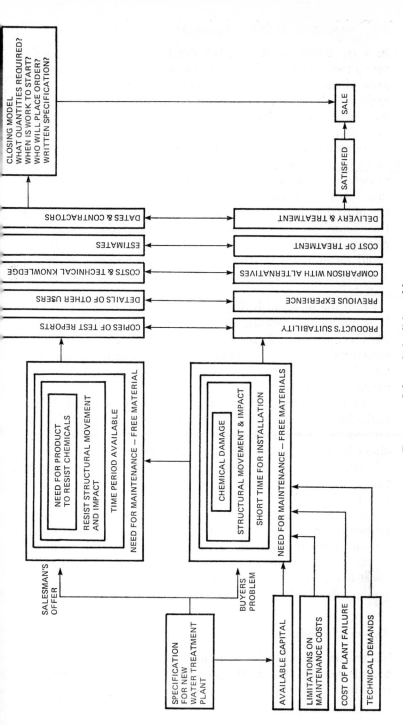

FIG. 24.—Salesman's implicit model.

its own structure in greater detail. The local authorities market will detail the limitations of authorities' spending power, area of operations, buying procedure, buying structure and their overall control. The re-organisation of local government will have made quite considerable revisions to this model a necessity.

Constructing a model differs in principle very little from steps taken in other forms of problem-solving. The first step is always to define the problem and to define the objectives in as much detail as possible in the form of a written statement. Defining the objectives is an important step in all situations calling for the commitment of resources. Any organisation must have clearly defined objectives to which it directs its efforts if it is to avoid meaningless progression of ideas. Before any course of action is initiated the objectives must be clearly determined and stated.

Once the problem is defined and the objectives determined it is possible to identify the central core of the problem. Management must then select the independent variables, those over which they have no direct control, and which in turn will affect the dependent variables over which management has some degree of control.

The relationships between the independent and dependent variables are examined and attempts made to explain the interrelationships. This can be used to construct a means/end chain in which one of the important dependent variables is selected and all the effects of each variable upon it examined in turn to discover what would happen if changes were to occur or could be induced.

Companies use models every day for a variety of control purposes. The company's organisation chart is a model of the formal authority structure. A profit and loss account is a model of the company's flows of revenue and costs. A break-even chart is a predictive model of the way in which a company's product should develop, produce cash and incur cash.

Types of model

There are three techniques in model construction. *Verbal* models are written descriptions of a problem or a market condition. *Graphical* models are diagrammatic representations

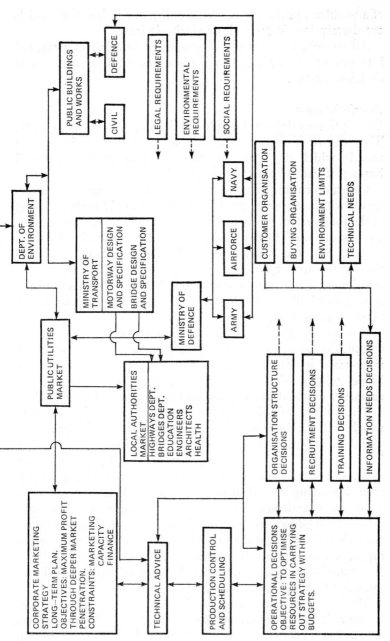

Fig. 25.—*Market structure model.*

of a problem, process or market condition. *Mathematical* models are descriptions in symbols or algebraic form.

All models, whether verbal, graphical or mathematical, fall into one of two broad classifications: descriptive models and decision models.

Descriptive models

Descriptive models are intended to show conditions as they are. They are designed to communicate an understanding of the way in which the system operates, and to predict what will happen if variables are manipulated.

Communication models describe the structural arrangements within a system, a set of blueprints to aid understanding of the total system by examining each part in turn. Explanatory models are used to describe the causal relationships between each set of elements in a system. Many economic models are of the explanatory type. Predictive models describe the causal relationships between a comprehensive set of elements in a system and indicate the degree of change likely to occur by the actions of any part.

It is possible to build descriptive models of different levels of complexity and incorporating varying degrees of detail. A *macro-model* illustrates a limited number of variables and the broad relationships between them. A sales manager might construct a model to show interactions in the volume of sales.

The volume of sales will be the single dependent variable which will be influenced by the effect of the independent variables including the level of national income, disposable income, wealth, the advertising messages that the population is exposed to and the average price level. Because such models only express inputs and outputs, stimuli and behaviour, without a necessary understanding of the decision-processes, they are called "black-box" models (*see* Fig. 26). The decision-processes are only inferred from the behaviour in response to a stimuli or input, *e.g.* a customer buys following exposure to advertising. If a sufficiently large population is involved then statistically some relationship exists but this is not understood.

Much of the model building in the field of consumer behaviour is based upon *micro-behavioural* models, themselves founded upon the "black-box" principle. A. E. Amstutz built a consumer model in which a population of potential buyers are

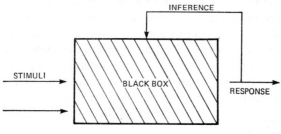

Fig. 26.—*Black-box model.*

subjected to weekly marketing stimuli and measures are taken of the fraction who purchase. Their purchases may be in direct response to the marketing stimuli but may also be the result of other stimuli.

Decision models
Decision models are intended to show how things should be and their purpose is to help evaluate the benefits of alternative courses of action. They may be either *optimisation* or *heuristic* models.

An optimisation model, generally used in operational research, is one for which computer programmes exist to find the best solution. A heuristic model has no computer programmes available to it, but it has the advantage of being more flexible. To use the model, the researcher applies heuristics, rules of thumb intended to shorten the time required to find a reasonable solution. These may amount to simple commonsense procedures used by the decision-maker in problem-solving. For example, faced with discovering concentrations of certain types of customers in the whole country, the rule of thumb might be to investigate only cities over 100,000 population.

Management faced with decisions need decision models and in day-to-day operations models such as break-even charts, pay-off cash flows and linear programming are used.

A wide variety of models are used in business today and will probably be used more widely in future. Like all marketing techniques, their use has both advantages and disadvantages.

Advantages include the clearer understanding of the problem and the interacting variables in a given situation. It is difficult to measure the value of the analysis process that has to be done by executives to agree on the interactions and variables but by focusing attention it forces management to clarify its ideas and often to go outside the immediate problem.

The disadvantages lie in the lengthy time needed to build a model which is characteristic of most operational research programmes. They are usually expensive to prepare and this must be offset against the benefits it is hoped will accrue. In all modelling there is the danger of over-simplification of the market situation.

Mathematical models of systems
In constructing a mathematical model of an interaction system, probability distribution of the variables is substituted for symbolic representations. By manipulating the model, outputs are produced and tested using standard performances as controls, or measured against existing performance levels. If it is shown that costs or efforts can be reduced then the solution is adopted as a new standard in place of existing practices.

Brand-switching and market-share models
A brand's market share comprises those purchasers who normally repeat their purchases of the brand from one week to the next, plus those purchasers who have changed their purchases from another competitive brand, less the previous purchasers who have switched to another brand. In simple terms it can be expressed as:

Market share = RB + SB(in) − SB(out), where RB are repeat buyers and SB are switch-buyers.

Marketing management's task is to increase the SB(in), which it endeavours to achieve through its communication system, sales force, sales promotion and advertising, pricing policy and distribution strategy.

In the mass markets for foodstuffs, household goods and other fast repeat purchase fields which have large enough populations to allow the use of statistical measuring techniques, the measurement of market share has been an area of growing importance.

The ability to measure brand loyalty effectively came with "preference analysis" developed by Audits of Great Britain Ltd. They provided the means of measuring accurately in terms of quantity, size of pack or money values, whereas before brand switching models had only been able to describe changes in the form of switching from one brand to another.

Brand-switching models are useful as techniques for explaining the effects of sales promotion, price changes or defensive advertising campaigns.

In brand switching the Markov-process model is perhaps most useful in describing a system in which the next state is influenced by the current state and also by a set of transitional probabilities. The fundamental principle of the Markov-process model is the state of the system. A system occupies a state when it is completely described by the values of variables that define the state.

"A system makes state transitions when its describing variables change from those specified for one state to those specified for another."

R. A. Edward, *Dynamic Programming and Markov-Processes*, The Technology Press and Wiley (copyright The M.I.T. Press), New York, 1960.

The system could be a group of consumers whose current state is the last brands purchased. The transitional probabilities would show the probability of a consumer passing from his current brand to any other available in the next period, as shown in Fig. 27.

Management science is concerned with the collection of consumer-panel data to indicate the choices made by consumers during successive time periods.

As an example we may consider consumer choice in purchasing three brands of washing powders, A, B and C. Of the consumers who previously purchased brand A, 75 per cent purchased it again; 15 per cent purchased brand B; 10 per cent purchased brand C. In this example brand A retained 75 per cent of its previous customers but lost 25 per cent with more going to brand B (15 per cent) than brand C (10 per cent). On this basis brand B is the greater competitive threat to brand A.

		Switch-buyers (in)		
		A	B	C
Switch-buyers (out)	A	75%	15%	10%
	B	20%	45%	35%
	C	4%	52%	44%

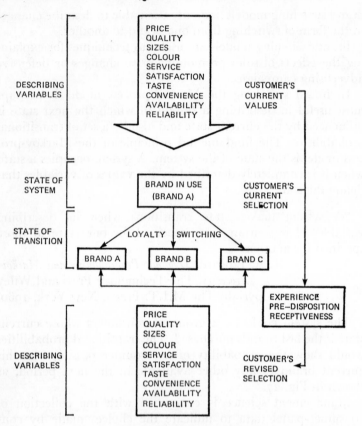

FIG. 27.—*Brand-switching transitional model.*

The matrix indicates where brand A former customers go and where the new customers originated. It suggests that as brand A receives 20 per cent of its customers from those lost by brand B, brand A and brand B are in close competition; it may well be a logical reaction by the manufacturers of brand A to consider some form of product differentiation.

A brand-switching model provides information about repeat buying rate, which is indicated by the diagonal numbers and also the rate of switching-in and switching-out for each brand along the lines of numbers.

As all brands in a market are affected to a similar degree by the state of system in terms of brand use and the state of transition, either by brand loyalty (repeat buying) or switching, it is possible to use the Markov-process in predicting long-range market shares. Compare this to the beer example of linear programming in Chapter 4. The matrix also indicates which brands offer the strongest competition and defence against attacks and which are vulnerable. It helps in forecasting both the magnitude and speed of change in market shares.

The ability to know the brands present market share to within fairly narrow limits and to be able to forecast likely trends with accuracy offers benefits to the company in being able to schedule production more accurately. This benefits the whole organisation and minimises losses from over- or under-production. There are savings to be gained from having less money tied up in stocks of both raw materials and finished goods. The company will also experience savings from being able to plan advertising campaigns more accurately.

Allocation models

Allocation models are an aid to the decision-maker to discover the best use of resources by allocating them so as to obtain the lowest cost or best return. They use the constraints imposed by production, marketing or the environment and express the objectives in mathematical form. Linear programming, discussed earlier in detail as a technique of operational research, is an allocation model.

Queueing or waiting-line models

These are designed to represent situations in which people or things are forced to wait. They seek to answer two questions: what length of waiting time may occur in a particular situation, and how will this waiting time be modified by changes in the facilities?

Queueing models have an obvious application in retail situations, supermarkets, petrol filling-stations, restaurants or railway ticket offices. They are useful in factory or college canteens to discover how many serving hatches and cash desks are required to obtain the optimum flow of customers.

In any situation where customers have to wait there is the danger that excessive waiting time will result in their moving to competitors.

Queueing models can be used when a hold-up will occur in the flow of materials as well as people. Enquiries received from

D

customers wait in turn to be answered, orders wait to be filled, materials queue to be used in production. In each waiting-time situation the problem has four dimensions; inter-arrival time, service time, the number of service facilities, *i.e.* check-outs, and the service method. Provision of too many check-outs will reduce the queue but incurs assets which may be under-utilised.

The length of a queue is a function of time and facilities in that they produce either an excess of waiting time or the facilities themselves are not adequate to the situation. Queueing models enable simulation of the problem facilitating collection of data derived from the arrival rate at the serving positions, the cost of maintaining these positions and their optimum throughout. In each case the constraints are the cost of providing a facility and the cost of lost sales.

Simulation models
Frequently the market situation is too complicated with too many variables interacting on the central problem to be represented by a standard mathematical formula. In these situations simulation offers a means of reproducing the situation in circumstances in which experimentation can take place to discover what will happen if variables are changed. It is a technique of dealing with complex processes. P. Kotler has commented:

"Simulation describes the act of creating a complex model to resemble a real process or system, and running and experimenting with the model in the hope of learning something about the real situation."

A scientist faced with decisions or questions in complex situations will begin by constructing a simple model that reproduces the conditions in a way that can be more readily understood. A scientist who wants to find out how a football will behave on a soccer pitch will begin by discovering how a billiard ball behaves on a smooth surface. An economist faced with problems of discovering how whole systems react to changes will experiment with small populations and measurable changes first. Doctor Barnes Wallis, when working on the special bombs needed to break the Moehne and Eder dams, wanted to find a way of ensuring the bombs would not be stopped by the torpedo nets which the Germans had strung across the water, and how he could make sure the bombs settled against the dam walls deep enough to produce the greatest shock waves. He found out initially by flicking ball bearings across a bath of water.

Simulation models adopt the same techniques of finding out what will happen in a complex situation by first experimenting with simple situations and building more complex models of the experience until as near real life as possible is achieved. Such a process is time-consuming and the greatest drawback to simulation models is the length of time needed for their construction and their cost. But as in most aspects of operational research and model building, they are only viable when the problem is large enough for the benefits to exceed the costs.

The immense problems incurred in exploiting oil resources produce such situations. How is the oil to be brought ashore? Methods of pipe laying and storage, distribution, queueing by tankers and lorries, supply to users and incoming supplies for use in the field, construction and operation of terminals are all areas for simulation modelling.

Enterprise models are used when it is required to know how the present enterprise utilises the flow of men, materials and finance and a model can show how changes might bring improvements.

Marketing-mix models are used to discover the effect different combinations of the marketing-mix will have upon a selected group or segment of the market. A hypothetical combination is selected and the reaction of customers is measured and then the combination is changed to see what effect alternative mixes might have.

Competition models are rather like a chess game. They are models intended to discover what happens if a course of action leads to a response by a competitor. Company A lowers their prices to increase market share; company B, whose production methods are known to be less efficient, cannot afford a long-term lowering of prices and therefore revenue, and they respond by a short-term sales promotion campaign aimed at attracting customers by a special offer and holding their loyalty afterwards. Company C, unable to do either, responds by improving his packaging and increasing price to suggest it offers a better quality product and appeals to a different group of customers.

Distribution channel models begin with transvections, *i.e.* diagrammatic representations of the flows incurred in getting products to consumers. Each individual exchange is a transaction and the total chain is a transvection. By examining the chain, marketing management can discover whether advantages will be obtained by changing the methods. These can be developed to include models of buyer demands in terms of discounts and costs, and buyer benefits in terms of distribution, savings in storage and promotional/selling facilities. Such a process is shown in Figs. 28 and 29.

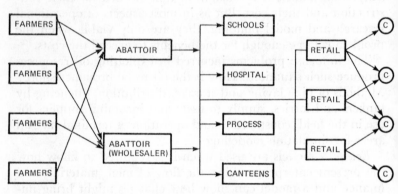

FIG. 28.—*Transvection model—general sales.*

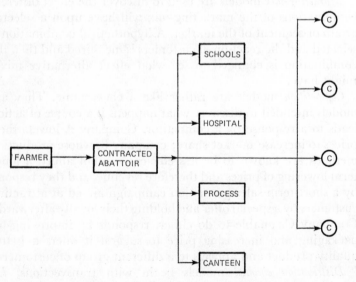

FIG. 29.—*Transvection model—direct sales.*

Models in corporate planning

Models have an important application to long-term corporate planning. To successfully plan by role a company must first become aware of its true nature. It should consider where its strength lies in terms of experience and its resources. A company has not only a fund of existing ability but also a depth gained by its operations over a period of time. It also has facilities which are likely to be adaptable to varying degrees and can be used for operations other than its current ones. In wartime many manufacturers of quality clothes become makers of uniforms or even parachutes. Companies making saucepans can quite easily make steel helmets or even weapons. Car manufacturers turn out tanks and aero-engines. In peacetime, faced with declining markets or economic pressures, firms seem atrophied and incapable of change. Planning by role rather than goal helps a firm to realise its long-term strategy, providing as it does for a built-in adaptability.

To plan by role, in the long term, the company must have a clear understanding of where it fits into the total field of operations and be able to react to changes in the environment. The discovery of oil in the North Sea and the prospects elsewhere have enabled some firms to change their operations without actually going outside their experience. A caterer on the East coast recognised the supply problems encountered by drilling rigs and drilling platforms and became a wholesale supplier to these structures with his own supply ships. Engineering works used to handling day-to-day industrial problems have adapted to the specialist needs of the developing industry. Hoteliers have seen the need for conference facilities close to the offshore operations and extended premises to provide for them.

A model to explore corporate identity must relate the company to its market and indicate the company's true nature and resources. It also has to reveal the nature of the company's competition and the economic pressures that will influence the environment. The type of model will vary greatly according to the business of the company, but its adaptability and certainty of application to each firm makes it a particularly effective tool of strategy. Models will necessarily vary according to the company and whether it is consumer-oriented or industrially-oriented.

To explore the company's role in a complex or technical field of industrial application requires the model to investigate what its particular skills fit it for apart from its existing production. Often a historical approach is helpful, especially when firms have had other forms of output in the past.

Such a company once sent a large number of its marketing staff to a course run by the author. It included directors, management and supervisory staff. The question posed for discussion was: What could the company do, apart from its present operations? It required course members to broaden their thinking, the original nine-dot puzzle application, and not be confined by what they took to be the only capability of the firm. A brains-storming session was inaugurated encouraging members to shout out any possibility that occurred to them. After a shaky start they entered into the spirit of the game.

The firm's current operation was in the field of air compressors and equipment based on the movement of air and fluids. As the session progressed the list of possibilities grew to include vehicles, military tanks, aircraft, aircraft systems, bakery equipment and so on. Afterwards the list was examined critically and with some humour until older members, looking back to the past, remembered that in wartime they had made parts for tanks, fluid movements systems for aircraft and that their air pressures systems had been incorporated into many different forms of production. Critically examined there were not many items of which the firm had no experience and with time, they could not become involved with once more. The model in Fig. 30, taken from *Sales and Sales Management* by P. Allen, represents some fields for expansion. It is not suggesting that the company tries all these.

A company that is aware of all possible areas of expansion is well placed to take advantage of any opportunities that might occur, for example, when it is announced that development work or contracts for some new technology project is being undertaken. The company that recognises its role can offer experience and skill and hopefully will already have done its own research, however preliminary.

In the example illustrated in Fig. 30, a firm in the technical field of compressors, looking for product diversification, cor-

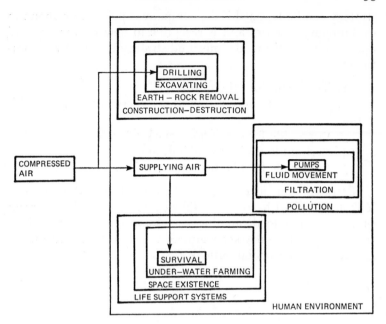

FIG. 30.—*Evolving corporate identity.*

porate expansion, or a strategy for the future will investigate
what it can do with existing skills apart from manufacturing air
compressors and equipment. The result of the modelling process may be the realisation that it does not have to search for
new products as it has not fully developed its existing skills.

The company, after exploring several alternative courses of
action, none of which goes outside its current technical expertise, then discovers it relates to three areas of development, each
concerned with changes in the human environment. It will
alert itself to any changes, government reports and economic
pressures that imply a need for skills in the pumping or storage
of air or fluids.

Having identified its true nature and accepted its role the
company can take quicker decisions as it is not moving out of
its field of experience or ability.

The key to long-term strategy is recognition of the company's
role and the business it is in. Graphic representations of the
company, its skills and environment in model form enable such
an examination to be fulfilled. The uncertainty of long-term

strategy can be lessened if the company is poised to respond to evolutionary changes and is receptive to new technology and opportunities. Our model must aid strategy to fulfil five conditions:

1. To extend into the future;
2. to take into account existing experience and capabilities;
3. to provide for continuous market reviews;
4. to simplify decision-making; and
5. to provide for planned opportunism.

If strategy can meet most of these conditions the firm can look forward with some confidence to maintaining current profits and not to dissipating its resources and energies in a thousand product–market ventures based on a limited understanding or a parochial outlook.

CHAPTER SIX

Market segmentation

The creation of markets

Marketing as a discipline has formed too recently to have evolved really sound deductive techniques, in which theorems can be evolved and tested by means of empirical evidence. There are, it is true, many theories relating to aspects of advertising, consumer behaviour and other behavioural studies within marketing. On the whole these theories have derived from the behavioural scientist casting his eye on marketing as an area to apply a general theory rather than marketing practitioners using the concepts of the psychologist or sociologist to aid his problem-solving. Often the result is a complicated explanation of a practice long used by marketing men.

In constructing a theory it is presumed virtuous to use a limited number of basic concepts. As one introduces more concepts it rapidly becomes difficult to explain their relationships and to produce a sound all-embracing theory.

In considering market segmentation, the purpose of which is fundamentally to create customers, we are concerned with behaviour systems and in particular *organised behaviour systems*. The marketing environment is composed of these entities in the same way as matter is composed of a variety of molecules and then atomic structures, the arrangement and relative numbers of which characterise the subject.

The nature of this environment is characterised by the *heterogeneous market*. A market that is perfectly heterogeneous is one in which there is a precise match between differentiated segments of demand and differentiated units of supply. It is important for marketing to accept the heterogeneity of the market so that stimulus is provided in the search for advantage over competitors. Among the diverse elements of the heterogeneous markets are to be found some with the characteristics most suited to the company's product range.

In accepting the state of the market as being heterogeneous, it must also be accepted that there are partial homogeneities to be found throughout the marketing system. Marketing aims to find partial homogeneities which have enough characteristics in common to form groups around which larger segments of the market may be formed by the influence of marketing communications. This phenomenon is illustrated schematically in Fig. 31. In general terms marketing comprises the activities of organised behaviour systems within heterogeneous markets.

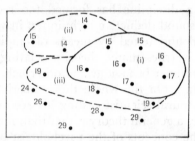

(a) *Homogeneity in teenage market for records:*
  (i) *First segment;*
  (ii) *extension of segment—younger;*
  (iii) *extension of segment—older.*

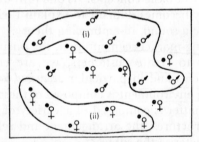

(b) *Homogeneity in same teenage market:*
  (i) *Segment 1—male teenage market, i.e. football wear;*
  (ii) *Segment 2—female young married market, i.e. baby goods.*

FIG. 31.—*Homogeneity in teenage market.*

The entire process of marketing, expressed in general terms, extends from the exploitation of conglomerate resources, limestone, timber, iron ore, to the end products in the hands of consumers, *i.e.* housing, furniture and newsprint, metal goods. Each step in the process is determined by the needs of particular segments of specific markets. The moving force for the whole process is the consumer, the intermediate exploitation and manufacturing processes are industrial and the final distribution is again to the consumer.

Markets which are defined as heterogeneous must also be regarded as discrepant. At any time consumers may demand products which are not available at that time. Equally, suppliers may endeavour to sell goods for which no demand exists. Any new product is in the last category and an important aspect of advertising is to bring together the two sides of the discrepant market. Given the circumstances in which markets are both heterogeneous and discrepant a potential exists for marketing management to exploit. The motivation which will result in a dynamic market is provided by expectations which exist within every organised behaviour system.

In a market that is discrepant it is possible for the discrepancy to be removed by one of two forms of innovation.

1. If consumers demand a product not currently available, it can be provided by innovation in production.

2. If a new product is created for which no demand exists, demand can be created by innovation in marketing, especially promotional activities.

Traditionally, totally homogeneous markets, even when discrepant, are not regarded as being dynamic. This is because in homogeneous markets the goods consumers demand are the same as those supplied. In the past, goods such as potatoes, paraffin and bread have been in this category. The packaging of potatoes, the branding and delivery of paraffin and the branding of bread have been successful attempts to introduce a differentiated product into homogeneous markets.

Markets have in the past been treated as collections of buyers who were not differentiated in their needs. This has led to a uniformity in production, distribution and sales in the belief that by adopting a low cost approach, consumers would more readily respond. The market for paraffin typified such a situation. The product was regarded as smelly, difficult to carry, unappealing, unidentifiable and was bought only be-

cause people with paraffin heaters had no option. Only when
brand names for paraffin were introduced could promotion and
communication aim messages at specific segments and try to
change attitudes towards their particular product. When
colouring was added to otherwise homogeneous products, consumers could actually look at paraffin and see the difference in
appearance. Promotion then added claims for individual products which may or may not have been as strong as suggested
but consumers were able to identify with their chosen brand.
When the door-to-door delivery services were started the product really began to compete.

There are important considerations to be drawn from the
realisation that markets are essentially heterogeneous and
discrepant. Such discrepancy may arise under conditions of
market expansion when new products may be sought, or under
conditions of market contraction when manufacturers may not
find customers for existing products. In a depression when
production of some goods may cease the two aspects of the
market are present.

Market imperfection arising from discrepancy creates a
dynamic and radical situation arising from demanded products
without supply and current products without demand. This
characteristic of marketing behaviour justifies its claim to be a
dynamic function which is expressed in four directions.

1. Creativity in product innovation;
2. creativity in marketing innovation;
3. its dynamic impact on its environment;
4. its influence upon marketing itself thereby instituting
change in functional behaviour.

In this chapter we are concerned with the first two, innovation in products and markets. This in itself depends upon the
products being aimed at the market with some precision, and
as in the example of the paraffin the search for differential
advantage.

A differentiated product is one in which there is some
feature which distinguishes it from all others. Examples from
present-day consumer advertising are:

". . . with the blue whitener." "With 10 per cent butter."
"With fluoride."

Such features may be trivial or significant but if it creates a loyalty among customers it is important as the reason for their purchase of that product in preference to other alternatives. Unless customers can readily distinguish the feature, that product has not fully entered into competition. No customer can consciously select a product by virtue of its difference unless he has a clear understanding of the ways in which it actually differs from alternatives. A manufacturer has a prime task to ensure his publicity and promotional activity fulfils the objective of registering these distinctions, otherwise his effort is wasted. If a manufacturer regards his market as homogeneous and therefore does not advertise or attempt to distinguish his product, then he is almost certain to fail.

The search for a differential advantage may be seen as the selection of strategies for achieving a desired market position. Originally the search for differential advantage was concentrated on the concept of product differentiation and only later was this search extended to the demand side. This search for a differential advantage on the demand side came from the realisation that heterogeneity existed in demand as well as supply, and was not necessarily a response to promotional activities by suppliers.

Market segmentation

[When the search for differential advantage is concentrated on the demand side it leads to market segmentation. The realisation that markets are not homogeneous but are made up of identifiable segments is critical to determining real marketing opportunities. It involves dividing the overall heterogeneous market into smaller homogeneous segments in order to be able to identify opportunities and needs and match them with precisely created products.]

Identification of groups of individuals with common characteristics does not necessarily constitute a marketing segment. It is only when these common characteristics relate them to their performance as buyers or consumers that a segment can be determined. For example a group of students may have many characteristics in common—age, outlook, general appearance or preferences in style of clothing—but none of these may be relevant to a company selling motor cycles.

Pertinent market segmentation exists when a product relates

strongly to certain consumers, but not to others; in fact when partial homogeneities exist. Studies of populations to highlight these partial homogeneities will frequently identify opportunities existing in a discrepant supply side of the market and may lead to innovation in new products. Such new products must have some unique feature which will make them clearly identifiable to the segment at which they are aimed.

The analysis of marketing segments is fundamental to marketing strategy; it is a reality that all managers should employ when making marketing plans with the aim of achieving optimum profits at minimum costs. There are two basic concepts involved.

First, the selection of marketing objectives requires an ability to measure effectively opportunities in different segments. Secondly, the ability to assess creatively the needs of different segments and apply the information to the selection of appropriate marketing-mix decisions.

Marketing segmentation begins with identifying customers' needs and interests, and the sub-dividing of a market into homogeneous sub-sets of customers which can be reached with a specific marketing-mix. The dynamic aspect of the concept is that in the intense competition for the mass markets individual manufacturers may achieve their objectives by concentrating on a segment of the total market whose needs are not entirely satisfied by the mass market suppliers. This happens in the paint market.

In a market dominated by industrial giants like Imperial Chemical Industries Limited, there are still around 4,000 companies in Britain producing paint. Many of these companies are selling to small segments, often too specialised for the giants to bother with. These small segments may be an area serviced by a local old established paint manufacturer, or a highly specialised product need of limited market size and commanding a high price.

When the author was in the surface coating industry he frequently won contracts from major industrial concerns for highly complex and costly treatments using products that were specially formulated or adapted. The larger paint companies, though technically competent, were not geared to producing this kind of low volume product. In a market dominated by supply contracts and lists of approved suppliers, the smaller manufacturer may not be able to get his price low enough to compete on general lines, but often there is a category of *special treatments* which are outside such approved lists and these small but highly lucrative segments offer great scope.

In this way segmentation has an impact upon the organisation and may lead to organisational development along the lines shown in Fig. 32.

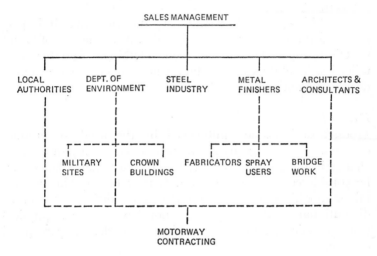

FIG. 32.—*Market segmentation—effect on sales organisation.*

Market segmentation as a policy has in the past originated with marketing research and its response was to produce separate versions of products to appeal to particular groups. A company producing menswear responded in this way.

The company's objective was to establish a market in West Germany. When sample suits were taken to German buyers, they were found to be unsuitable and extensive design modifications had to be carried out. With the redesigned suits the company began to look for customers, other than West German, who would buy the new suits.

This situation meant that companies often found that the existence of these distinctions between customers, *i.e.* British and West German, did not always reflect their buying behaviour in respect of individual products. While German menswear buyers in department stores reflected the known mass demand among their customers it did not follow that the customers themselves could not be motivated to buy different styles if they were given the opportunity.

It is this kind of situation which led marketing men to consider other forms of segmentation analysis, apart from the marketing research–product oriented approach. Among the techniques developed has been consideration of *personality variables*, which have been employed to segment confectionery markets.

Advertising men have long held the view that it is personality differences between people that lie at the root of brand selection, especially among food, clothing, cigarettes and toiletries. All of these are products where advertising uses a high degree of emotional appeal.

Product policy

Product decisions are influenced by the needs of product changes. The change itself can be defined as any discernible change in the product as viewed by the customer. Change can be considered in different ways. It may be anything from a minor modification to extensions of the existing range or its discontinuance. A change does not have to be a physical characteristic but may be nothing more than a perceptual change.

Perceptual changes can result from promotional activity intended to change the way people think about a product. One of the greatest perceptual changes by promotional means was the result of the Esso Petroleum Company's "Tiger in the Tank" campaign. There the perceptual change was away from the technical merits of petrol buying to the fun aspects and away from the traditional petrol buyer segment, the driver, to his children. The children influenced his, the driver's, purchases by wanting the Tiger accessories—tail badges, tee shirts and so on. It was probably the most successful campaign ever run.

Such a promotional effort is not wholly a segmentation policy but owes as much to a policy of product differentiation. It aims to make a non-differentiated product different in the eyes of consumers.

Another example of this policy is the marketing of tile adhesives. This product was sold to builders and contractors at more or less the same price and discounts as competitors;

quality was simply a matter of sticking on a tile. It was very difficult to establish a brand image or loyalty until the manufacturer hit on the idea of packing the adhesive into plastic buckets instead of cans. In buying the adhesive the builder had a ready supply of handy buckets.

We can distinguish between product differentiation and market segmentation in this way:

Differentiation is the blending of market requirements to existing products and segmentation is the adaptation of the product to different market requirements.

From this one can see it is largely a matter of which end of the product/market process is tackled.

Benefits from market segmentation

Marketing management will only undertake segmentation policies if it can be shown that benefits will accrue to the company. There are four areas of benefits derived from segmentation:

1. The company will be able to identify marketing opportunities more quickly and by a process of comparison and evaluation, select policies which will benefit the company over the longest period of time.

2. The company is able to plan more effectively by concentrating its research and planning in limited segments and thereby allocate resources more effectively.

3. The company can direct its promotional activities more accurately at the characteristics of each segment.

4. It will be able to undertake longer-term product planning by concentrating upon product/market segments of which it has greater experience.

A company that has a continual market segmentation policy is able to measure and monitor current competitive activity as a gauge for its own activities. Any segment not subject to strong activity can be considered a possible area for profitable operation.

In carrying out a policy of market segmentation, marketing management has to be aware of its limitations and the likely problems that can be encountered.

The seller's problem is to determine which buyer's characteristics are likely to create the correct segmentation within a particular market. In selecting characteristics for segmentation three criteria must be applied:

1. *Measurability:* the degree to which the company is able to collect information of a measurable nature.

2. *Accessibility:* the degree to which a company can apply its marketing effort to a selected segment; how far does the existing media offer access to the segment?

3. *Substantiality:* are the selected segments large enough or profitable enough to merit consideration as a separate segment? As a guide, the segment should be the smallest unit for which justification can be made for separate marketing programmes.

It must be said that in the economic crisis at the time of writing, the units of markets must grow larger as the potential for small segments becomes less and they are aggregated to a profitable level. Segmented marketing is expensive and in a period of falling demand levels of profitability must also fall. The aggregation of segments will lead, hopefully, to increased profitability but must inevitably limit consumer choice.

Cost of segmentation

Segmentation is frequently used in consideration of marketing cost analysis. In particular an understanding of segmentation and decision-making is desirable on subjects such as:

1. Allocation of salesmen's effort within different marketing segments;
2. allocation of costs to different sized territories;
3. profitability of different types of customers;
4. feasibility studies on products to be sold.

Commencing with a total marketing budget, marketing management is concerned with the allocation of costs to different strategies, a marketing-mix determination problem. The overall budget will be sub-divided into budgets for the different functional activities, such as personal selling, marketing research, distribution, pricing, advertising, etc. A sub-budget for the export department would have to be in the light of decisions for the allocation of funds for their particular forms of business, customers, products or market segments. In decisions regarding, for example, either the Belgian market or the

Egyptian market, the level of optimisation required does not alter the fundamental rule that the MRP/MRC (marginal revenue product/marginal revenue cost) ratios must tend to equality in the longer term.

In the hypothetical example of the export decision, management is concerned with the effective employment of personnel and resources for different market segments. The MFC (marginal factor cost) of employing resources in either market is the compensation to staff, interest on capital employed, or even a costing on the time employed per order or visit to the market. The MRP of the resources employed is the unit sales per visit or unit of time, etc., (marginal physical product) times the unit price of such sales (marginal revenue). Expressed simply a decision to exploit one segment in preference to another is the level of profitability (P) between them on the basis of:

$$P = MFC - MRP \ (MPP \times MR)$$

Product life-cycles

Marketing segmentation aids management in maximising the return on its investment in products and in production. Marketing executives, like other functional executives, are very dependent for their decision-making upon the quality of their information, quite often they receive too little too late. Marketing as a function is concerned above all else with communication and it is a paradox that so much marketing effort fails because of limitations in its communication system. Information is frequently collected, or already exists, but it is not communicated to the essential point of decision-making. Much of the information is decentralised and while it exists somewhere in the organisation, it is unverified and frequently goes to the wrong person.

Marketing information falls into one of two broad classifications:

1. *Situational information,* which describes the nature of the subject in general terms leading to its analysis, and including marketing surveys, product specifications, and competitor activities which improve management's understanding.

2. *Dynamic information,* which determines the changes in the system, either by trend information on market growth or technical developments, or variance information which

provides a comparison of actual performance against a control and has as its main purpose the provision of cues for actions, and permits a better timing of decisions.

Market segmentation, if it is to be useful, must reflect marketing management's appreciation of the situation, trends and developments. The product life-cycle is a useful concept in achieving such an understanding.

All products are subject to constant change, an erosion of their original specification and purpose, from the moment they are launched. As they go through different stages in their life-cycle so they become subject to varying strategies aimed at a changing appreciation of their relationship to the market.

Fig. 33 is a simplified product life-cycle showing two main features. The unit sales curve typically jumps on introduction, as customers buy the product experimentally. This is generally followed by a levelling off while it is evaluated, the period depending on the use to which the product is put. Once initial purchases have been evaluated the unit sales curve grows steadily through the growth phase to the maturity phase, when the product is widely accepted, and so into saturation. At this point all additional sales have to be won with increasing effort; it is a phase at which market forcing becomes important.

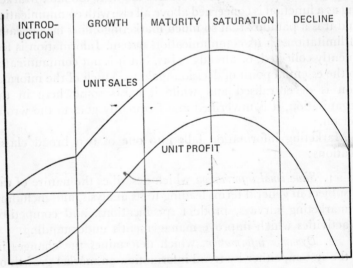

FIG. 33.—*Simplified product life-cycle.*

Eventually the product declines as later versions come on to the market, or competition is too strong.

In retrospect most firms know what happened to their product from launch to withdrawal. They can deduce this information from the records of unit sales. Unfortunately unit sales are not the complete story, as it is unit profit which is the important guide but is not always recorded accurately.

At launch the product is costed accurately on the basis of product costs plus selling costs. Initially these are not likely to vary with any significance. But when the product is proving successful competitors enter the market, sometimes, though not always, with a slightly cheaper product. With a competitor in the field the original firm will have to respond to hold its market share by improving deliveries, more sales calls, more advertising, promotions, etc. These extra expenditures are costs which are not all attributable to the product with any accuracy. The result is that long before unit sales are noticeably falling, unit profit has already fallen. As competition grows so costs increase until products are selling at a loss. This is not automatically a situation in which the product is dropped, however, as will be seen from further discussion of other aspects of the product life-cycle in Chapter 8.

The importance of the product life-cycle to market segmentation is that as the phases of the cycle change so the product becomes suited to a different segment of the market and to differing strategies. It is, then, important to examine the product life-cycle and its effect upon planning strategies in order to understand market segmentation, in particular, the influence of product life-cycle pressures and those of competitors which create the need for segmentation.

A. Patton, of McKinsey & Co., determined that in the *introductory* phase the essential management skill lies in being able to develop the market and the product concurrently. It represents the importance and the dynamic element of the discrepant market concept. A new product launched at an unprepared market is a seed on stony ground, while a prepared market for which no product is readily available represents a waste of resources and may be harmful to future plans.

Mickwitz, commenting upon the introduction phase, suggested that it is the level of quality which has greatest impact. Early products are often poor in performance and are replaced as better quality products take over, often at a higher price. This is true of new types of product, whether washing machines or instant mashed potato.

Having successfully launched the product, Patton suggests that management must go for volume in the growth phase, which will lower production costs, and if these can be passed on to the customers in lower prices it will encourage further consumption and strengthen the company against the effects of competition. The strategy for achieving volume will include advertising of consumer goods and personal selling of industrial goods. This strategy also ensures that early buyers of the product become committed to it and the sampling process is turned into repeat volume business.

Perhaps the biggest example is the way in which the American aircraft industry launches new military aircraft. Once the experimental aircraft has been proved, the company will go all out for an order for the United States Air Force which will enable the company virtually to recover its development costs and then undersell its European rivals.

Many companies fail to make sufficient impact on the market at this stage and establish themselves soundly before competitors can catch up. The American Kodak–Eastman Company did when it launched its Instamatic camera simultaneously in twenty-six major cities worldwide and established a lead that its competitors took two years to reach, by which time Kodak had moved on.

According to Mickwitz, the first signs of market segmentation appear in the maturity phase. At this point in the cycle competition becomes much stronger and some companies may attempt to pull in the price sensitive segments of the market by lowering prices. With many competitors the company must ensure that customers recognise its products and understand the benefits. It will achieve this aim by implementing strategies of aggressive and informative advertising to consumer markets, and creative selling to industrial markets.

It is during the maturity phase that segmentation often proliferates (*see* Fig. 34), pricing and advertising each tending to appeal to different groups of customers. Frequently at this stage products can be developed to appeal to different groups, leading to re-cycle phases, with identifiably modified products.

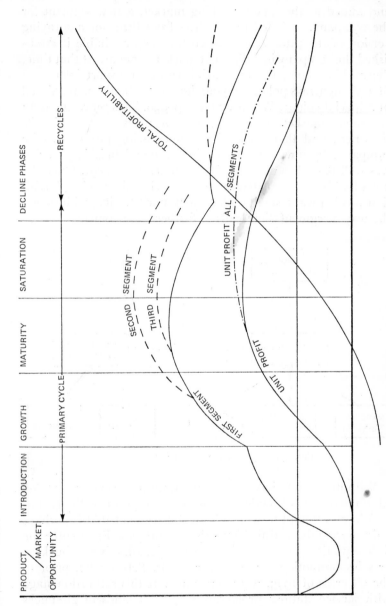

Fig. 34.—*Effect of segmentation on the product life-cycle.*

In the surface coating field a metallic coating was introduced and aimed at the metal finishing market, a new segment for the company. This led to enquiries from firms for a spraying version of the product and when that was available it established the company in a different market segment. At that time, the middle 1960s, the then Ministry of Transport instructed that all highways poles, carrying signs, etc., should be repainted in a special colour, Warboy's Grey 9–096. This represented an enormous market with thousands of poles needing *in situ* treatment and thousands of new ones being produced. The company, by now experienced in the metal finishing market was well placed to exploit this new market segment. Once the poles had been completed the segment virtually vanished as all that was left was a small replacement market. Fig. 35 illustrates the way a segmentation leads to further development.

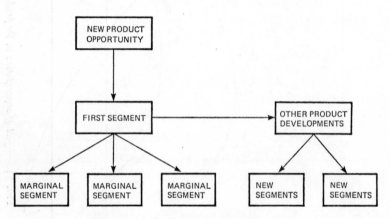

Fig. 35.—*Segmentation and product development.*

With many suppliers in the market, supply becomes *saturated*. Manufacturers will endeavour to increase product differentiation in an attempt to win a share of a segment that is perhaps only marginally satisfied by existing supplies. Frequently the differentiation is in non-product terms, *i.e.* adhesives in buckets, or sales promotion for consumer goods. Petrol sales, prior to the oil crisis of 1973, were very much at this saturation stage with service stations proliferating and all kinds of gimmicks being used to extend appeal to segments other than the driver.

Frequently there will be a strong emphasis on service which

is an expensive addition and depresses unit profits still further.

The final phase of the primary cycle is *decline*. Market demand eventually falls away in response to diminishing returns to promotional efforts and aggregate competition. Pressures on costs become greater and the company seeks ways to save. In labour-intensive industries, like clothing, companies may simply drop the product and use their resources to make something else. Capital-intensive industries will not be able to recombine their resources in the short term and instead will go for volume at any price so long as some contribution is made to their direct costs. It is the phase of price wars when quality drops and worn-out plant is not replaced.

Each phase of the product life-cycle presents a choice of decisions on segmentation. But at each stage there are strategies for getting the most out of existing markets. It may be by encouraging more frequent use of the product among existing customers, or by developing different uses for the product among existing customers. Alternatively the company may develop sales to new markets, for example, exporting.

These three strategies extend the life of the products in a way that has been termed a "re-cycle," although it is possible to argue that the "re-cycle" is really only an integral part of the product's life-cycle. Life-cycles generally have been shorter since marketing has encouraged people to replace their consumer durables more rapidly, although there are products which appear to go on indefinitely.

The trend has been to quicker response by competitors, rapid technological development and a smaller level of segmentation making for a wider variety of ranges. Market segmentation has encouraged this process, although the economic reversals of the seventies would appear to have reversed the process for the moment.

Marketing management on the whole needs to base its strategy on the understanding that it is not possible to please everyone with the same product. Total product offerings are thereby adapted to the demands of relatively homogeneous groups through the segmentation process.

Segmentation and attitude
We have seen that because of the ways in which products at various stages in their developments interact with the market a

process of segmentation is inevitable. Management's problem is not whether to segment, in that there is no choice, but rather how to maximise the results. The search to make one product different from competing products which all have the same basic characteristics is one of the strongest elements in present-day marketing strategy.

The demands of modern production methods result logically in market aggregation, that is, a policy of trying to satisfy the whole market with the smallest number of products. This is in contrast to marketing's strategy of trying to develop products to meet the desires of specific groups. Somewhere between these two extremes is the optimum level of market segmentation.

It is not sufficient in segmentation policy to know which products are most acceptable in the market but rather to discover which characteristics of the product are preferred and which are disliked. If marketing is to be dynamic it must develop a capability to change attitudes and not simply respond to them.

Research into consumer behaviour should try to understand the distribution of preferences for a variety of characteristics in order to predict the size of a segment for products possessing a given characteristics-mix. Only such a process of research, application and analysis can provide a meaningful basis for market segmentation which is developed from an appreciation of customer attitudes.

Once the distribution of customer preferences is known they can be matched with the segmentation characteristics, *i.e.* demographic, social or behavioural, of the population. From this it becomes possible to isolate the groups to which the marketing efforts can be most profitably directed.

Given the situation in which an identified set of preferences cannot be built satisfactorily into the product's characteristics, marketing management is faced with a problem. It is accepted that human beings will resist a challenge to their attitudes and a product that does not accord to consumer attitudes is likely to be rejected. In spite of their resistance to change, people are not totally impermeable in their attitudes and marketing communications (advertising, sales promotion and selling) are all undertaken with the aim of persuading people to modify their preferences and buying behaviour.

Marketing management will want to avoid attempting to

change attitudes in those segments where the probability of change is low and will allocate resources to segments where probability of change is high. The question then becomes: Under what circumstances is attitude change most likely to occur? What are the determinants of attitude strength?

As a general rule the probability of change varies inversely with strength of attitude. The stronger is the customer's predisposition, the less is the probability that the attitude will give in under persuasive communication inputs. The underlying reasons for attitude strength are four-fold.

1. Attitudes are more susceptible to change as a result of contradictory information if the existing knowledge is small.

2. Attitudes which are intimately related to the subject's self-concept, *i.e.* having centrality, are most resistant to change, and represent important motivation values.

3. It is difficult to change attitudes that are highly interconnected with other attitudes. Human beings tend to strive for balance in their attitudes and a move in one attitude will usually lead to change in others. Change is resisted when these interconnections are high.

4. Personality will affect resistance to change to a high degree. People with strong beliefs are less likely to change attitudes in response to incoming information than people with no strong beliefs.

The strongest element in the four determinants is a strong commitment to a particular viewpoint. Resistance to change is closely related to the commitment factor and people who do not have strong commitments will assimilate incoming information more readily.

This factor of commitment is important in understanding attitudes to advertising and other marketing communications. There is evidence to show that consumers who are strongly committed to a preference in products become dissonant when that preference is seemingly challenged.

In the measurement of commitment, brand loyalty, product or store loyalty, are all commitments of importance to marketing. A company opens a branch store in a town; it directs its merchandising policy towards those segments it believes will respond to its particular range of appeals. The difficulty lies in measuring the level of commitment by consumers. Most attitude measurements refer only to a single point on a scale of effects and many would question whether this is valid for measures of consumer behaviour as a guide to market segmentation.

Two individuals may be equally predisposed to a brand of foodstuffs. One considers no alternative brands to be acceptable while the other has no such categorical conviction. While each is favourably disposed it is not true that they have an equal commitment.

C. W. Sherif, M. Sherif and R. E. Nebergall in *Attitude and Attitude Change: The Social Judgement-Involvement Approach* (Philadelphia, W. B. Saunders, 1965) found that there is a range of positions from acceptable to unacceptable which is the key to determining the individual's strength of commitment. They proposed as being of special importance two scales of measurement:

1. Latitude of acceptance;
2. latitude of rejection.

According to Sherif, Sherif and Nebergall, "the latitude of acceptance includes both the most acceptable position on the issue as well as others that are accepted. The latitude of rejection, on the other hand, embraces the most objectionable position towards the same phenomena plus other objectionable positions."

This concept still leaves the possibility of positions that are neither acceptable nor rejected. Sherif suggested this as a latitude of non-commitment.

Up to the present, research suggests that the degree of commitment can be measured operationally by a process of comparing the number of positions on the various latitudes. If a person is strongly committed to a product, there is a greater extent of levels of rejection relative to the latitude of acceptance, while the area of non-commitment is almost nil. The measurement of commitment offers an operational means of study provided the researcher is able to determine a basis of measurement.

Once commitment has been assessed marketing management can plan its communications effectively to induce a change in attitude. Market segments which are strongly committed to another brand, will not be ideal targets for utilisation of promotional resources.

Producing attitude change

Management's problem is to determine the strength of commitment and isolate market segments which will offer a high probability of producing a change in attitude, and determine the methods to be pursued.

"The type of message that is likely to be most effective in inducing attitude change is one well tailored to fit the particular attitude structure, being relevant to the motivational bases of the attitude, yet involving arguments that are sufficiently novel that it is unlikely the individual is already fortified with counter information."

T. M. Newcomb, R. H. Turner and P. E. Converse,
Social Psychology, Holt, Rinehart & Winston Inc., 1965.

As was mentioned above, human beings tend to strive for balance in their attitudes, so that a change in one attitudinal dimension will lead to a corresponding change in others. A variety of approaches to attitude change can be undertaken.

The company may provide new information that will add to, and change the cognitive dimension. It may change the way in which people think about the product, *i.e.* Honda motor cycles, soft margarine, soft drinks in screw-top bottles.

It may aim to add to information that will associate the end state of change with the desirable consequences, *i.e.* hair-sprays, deodorants, floor cleansers.

The company may undertake some form of advertising that will contradict the recipients' normal behaviour, changing the behavioural dimension, *i.e.* safety at work, persuade people to stop smoking.

There is a definite correlation between the repetition of an advertising message and buying activity. A company that understands the distribution of preferences and incorporates them into the product, and determines the most receptive market segments, can motivate potential customers to buy through persuasive advertising. It must be stressed that persuasive advertising is as much dependent upon identifying and understanding segments of its audience as the client manufacturer is, if it is to achieve a high degree of effectiveness. In industrial marketing, where the role of advertising is limited, personal selling must undertake the task of changing attitudes.

For more detailed explanation of these methods, readers are recommended to the M & E Handbook, *Sales and Sales Management*, by P. Allen.

Marketing, contrary to popular belief, is not capable of changing customers' behaviour if by that is meant causing people to do something contrary to their predisposition when they are strongly committed. It has been suggested that one can only change people's behaviour if one can directly control the subject's environment as in the political field.

Brand loyalty has long been regarded as useful in formulating marketing strategy, especially in consumer markets. In concept brand loyalty is a way of achieving market segmentation but in practice it is so difficult to identify specific differences between people buying different brands that it becomes impossible to form identifiable segments.

Bases of segmentation
There are problems in finding rational bases for segmentation whether industrial or consumer. The initial segmentation is itself a distinction between industrial goods and consumer goods.

Traditionally consumer markets have been segmented along *demographic* dimensions, such as age, sex, income, family size, occupation and social class. As mentioned in the paragraph on implications of brand loyalty, it is difficult to identify specific differences in this way. Many argue that as demographic methods fall short as a means of segmentation markets should be analysed to detect *personality* values, gregariousness, attitude, authority style, ambition, and differences in motivation. Other segments are by *geography*: regions, area, size of city or climate.

Industrial segments are generally more clearly definable, but often the segment is limited to only a few companies. Common bases are: geographical, industrial, types of business, purchasing patterns and size.

English Clays, Lovering and Pochin Limited analyse market segments in order to estimate the size of their market:

"By analysing the individual sectors of the market in some detail and taking into account the various trends, influences and expectations, we have forecast the likely level of demand up to 1974. In the last analysis, however, this forecast like any other, depends on judgement and as such it represents our best efforts to interpret and project a complex, difficult and variable market."

The United Kingdom Market for Coated Printing Papers, 1968–74, English China Clays Sales Company Limited.

Table XIII is reproduced from the above publication and shows how the analysis was used to produce an estimated forecast of the consumption of coated printing paper in 1974 as being 420,000 (long) tonnes. Recently the results were confirmed as follows, quoted from a letter from Mr. D. A. Clark, the General Marketing Manager.

TABLE XIII. *Forecast consumption of coated printing papers in 1974 by end-use.*

End-use	1968 000 tonnes	1974 000 tonnes	% increase 1968–74	per annum
Publishing				
Trade and technical journals	66	88	33·3	5·0
Consumer magazines	33	38	18·2	3·0
Part publications	8	23	187·5	19·0
Books and directories	20	27	35·0	5·0
Total	127	177	39·4	5·7
Advertising				
Mail order catalogues	23	33	43·5	6·5
Direct mail and trade catalogues	20	35	75·0	10·0
Holiday and travel literature	14	22	57·1	7·5
Other advertising literature	55	73	32·7	5·0
Total	112	163	45·5	6·5
Labels and wrappers	40	54	35·0	5·0
All other uses	18	26	44·4	6·0
Total	297	420	41·4	5·9

"Incidentally your letter prompted me to check the accuracy of our forecast for 1974 with the actual results which are now becoming available. Our estimate was a total consumption of 420,000 (long) tonnes in 1974 while actual results indicate an apparent consumption of 470,000 (metric) tonnes. However, as the paper industry is now learning to its sorrow, 1974 was an abnormal year with a considerable build up in stocks which are now being worked off. Real consumption of coated paper in 1974 is estimated at between 420,000 tonnes and 430,000 metric tonnes which is very gratifying to us." July, 1975.

Segmentation and strategy
Fig. 36 represents four marketing situations which management must consider in assessing its strategy for market segmentation.

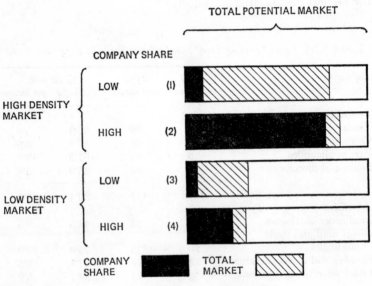

FIG. 36.—*Allocation of marketing effort.*

In situations (1) and (3) there is potential for growth as the company has only a small share of the market. In market situation (1) there is little remaining potential and any growth will have to be achieved through stressing product differences and advantages to persuade consumers to buy the company's product in preference to those of alternative supplies. Since the market is almost totally served, competitors will soon become aware of what is happening as they lose their share of the market, and will respond with appropriate promotional policies. In situation (3) growth can be achieved from the large potential remaining and the company will attempt to expand into untouched segments by assisting the total market to grow.

Market situations (2) and (4) represent conditions in which the company has a high share of the existing market. Market (2) offers little potential as the company dominates the market and there is little potential remaining. In such conditions the company's strategy will be defensive as its competitors can grow only at the expense of the market leader.

Market situation (4) is the most dynamic situation for the company as it has a large share of a market with considerable growth potential. It will undertake activities that will encourage expansion into other segments and will encourage greater use among existing users.

When marketing management has discovered the best method of segmenting the market, whether consumer or industrial, the process will become a basis for all other marketing evaluations. Marketing segmentation is a strategy of divide and rule enabling better product planning, more rational selling operations and the setting of precise and measurable marketing objectives.

E

CHAPTER SEVEN

Performance evaluation

The central problem of ensuring that adequate performance is maintained lies in the creation of logical and dynamic organisation structures. Business organisations, like other forms of organisation in non-business areas, *e.g.* teaching, or hospitals, are made up of varying numbers of people organised to carry out tasks that have been allotted to them in accordance with predetermined standards.

In non-business areas the process of change is normally in response to internal pressures for rationalisation as perceived by the organisation or some body of control. An example of this is the way the army amalgamates units to fulfil the government objective of saving costs. It is usually a deliberate policy phased over a period of time.

Business firms are working in an environment over which they have minimum control in conditions of imperfect knowledge. Response, therefore, is frequently a matter of adaptation to a form more suited to the changed circumstances at a particular point in time, but which will no doubt change again.

In marketing the organisational problem is yet more acute, as the need to respond to change must be recognised more quickly than in other functions which depend upon marketing for information. There is an immediate problem in the marketing function of determining the relationship between sales and marketing. There are three basic alternatives in which the choice should be a matter of analysing how far each possibility is most suited to the functional objective:

1. Adopt marketing as the functional title and limit the responsibilities of sales to those activities related to selling and the sales office, as in Fig. 37.
2. Adopt sales as the functional title where the activities

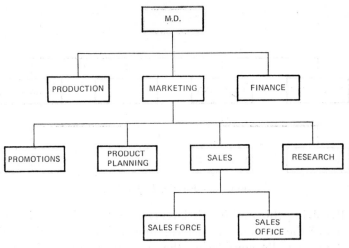

FIG. 37.—*"Marketing" as functional title.*

are directly involved in, and limited to, the selling process, as in Fig. 38.

3. Distinguish between sales and marketing at the functional level, sales containing those activities related to the selling process and of a tactical nature, with marketing responsible for the strategic activities as in Fig. 39.

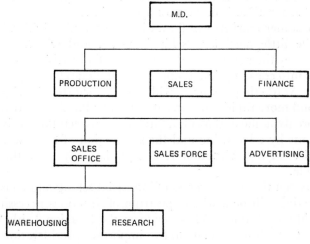

FIG. 38.—*"Sales" as functional title.*

FIG. 39.—*Functional separation.*

Resolving this problem is largely a matter of analysing the needs of the market and determining how the objectives will best be met. By considering the cost effectiveness of various marketing-mix alternatives a set of marketing activities will result, an analysis of which will indicate, if not positively determine, the functional title.

In the industrial market, cost effectiveness will result in emphasis upon personal promotion and communication. This entails a high level of training in the sales force, technically competent and backed by a strong servicing activity. Marketing research will tend to be a long-term process and the role of advertising limited. In this situation choice 3, Fig. 39, functional separation, is often most appropriate.

Consumer markets call for a different set of activities. There will be little need for "selling" as demand will largely be created by the non-personal promotion of advertising "pulling" goods into consumption as opposed to the sales force "pushing" them. Marketing research will need to shorten its sights to respond more rapidly to consumer trends. Physical distribution is more dynamic and forms a vital link between the motivation of wants by advertising and the satisfaction of those wants by impulse buying. Situation 1, Fig. 37, is likely to be the most suitable.

Between the two extremes of industrial selling and consumer marketing will be a whole spectrum of situations necessitating individual solutions. Whatever form the functional title eventually takes, it must relate to two important considerations: the creation and maintenance of satisfied customers, and the fundamental business objective which is to make a sale. Too often marketing is equated with a range of skills and techniques for understanding customers, and this omits the most important end which is selling products.

Any organisation which exists to create customers must be capable of fully utilising the skills at its disposal. Any product will remain the result of design and productive skills unless the total resources available to management can be combined to transform the basic idea into a concept that accords to customers' needs. But the achievement of the product's sale must be at an acceptable cost if it is to contribute to the company's revenue and growth.

Organisation and marketing

It has already been established that if marketing is to ensure its success it must be responsive to changes in its environment. A fundamental response is that of looking to its organisation, ensuring it is adequate to meet the tasks before it. If organisation has developed haphazardly or is slow to respond to change then anomalies will arise and its effectiveness will be less than maximum. To ensure that the function performs efficiently, therefore, a continuing review of the organisation is essential, not only to avoid having activities and posts that are no longer necessary but more important to make sure that those remaining are staffed by the correct personnel with appropriate training and motivation. While this is most obvious in the sales force it is essential throughout the function.

Organisation has been defined by Milward as follows:

"Organisation is a process of dividing work into convenient tasks or duties, of grouping such duties in the form of posts, of delegating authority to each post, and of appointing qualified staff to be responsible that the work is carried out as planned."

Douglas MacGregor, writing on the organisation, said: "The personalities of the men who control enterprises have a profound effect upon the efficient operation of it."

These two quotations express important concepts for marketing organisation. First, that one appoints *qualified* staff able to carry out the work as planned, and, secondly, that the personalities of those who control have a profound effect.

If we ensure that the personnel appointed are suitably qualified the element of control has a changed role. Control over unqualified staff means ensuring they do the job adequately, while control over trained and qualified personnel is largely a matter of ensuring they act on a co-ordinated basis within the framework of company policy. On the one hand a certain amount of coercion, on the other a need for communication. Get the wires crossed and trouble inevitably results.

Organisation structures also define the responsibilities and formal relationships throughout the enterprise and are normally stated in the form of schedules of responsibilities. In *Sales and Sales Management* it was stated: "It is reasonable to say that an obtuse tidyness of mind can have disastrous effects if applied too rigidly to a highly competitive environment such as that in which the modern business firm competes." To operate effectively organisation must allow the dynamic initiative which is essential in today's changing world.

Organisation theory which is applied too rigidly can result in doctrinaire practices based more on theoretical validity than market pressures. C. S. Deverell, in *Business Administration and Management*, puts it succinctly: "An excessive specialisation planned on doctrinaire lines in a rigid functional structure can provide a disastrous case history of valid theory unintelligently applied."

Similar enterprises may have comparable patterns of delegation and two companies launching competitive products in the same market at the same time may well begin operations with the same form of organisation. But practice in the market, and most important the dynamic processes of differentiation and segmentation (*see* Chapter 6), will begin to change the organisation as it evolves to meet each new opportunity. Each market segment represents a micro-environment and success may depend on adapting to it.

Charles Darwin evolved his theory of natural selection after his voyage in the *Beagle* took him to the many small islands of the Galapagos group. There he found species of finches living among the islands. Although they had many common features and clearly had originally been of one species, the finches on each island had evolved slightly different features as an adaptation to the small environmental differences of each island.

 Marketing is a dynamic area and must be prepared to adapt on the basis of constantly changing and evolving conditions where micro-environments spring up, mature and fade away. From this one can see a market life-cycle comparable to the product life-cycle and calling for different management styles. In this way the firm will be able to construct an organisation capable of adaptation and able to fulfil its needs at a particular time and from then after, constantly review the operating conditions.

Organisation and goals

Organisation must be related to goals. Where the purpose is profit the structure must allow individuals to develop ideas and abilities which will aid corporate development. In an organisation in which there are non-profit objectives the system may be mechanistic and personal limitations may lead to frustration if individual goals and ambitions are not capable of realisation.

In *Sales and Sales Management* it was suggested that there exists two basic organisation structure types:

1. Profit-centred organisation; and
2. community-centred organisation.

By considering the nature and objectives of the organisation we can make certain assumptions which will aid understanding of personnel considerations in organisation.

Type A—Profit-centred organisation:

1. The business organisation's survival is directly related to profitability;

2. the organisation must be adaptable to the changing needs of the environment and have no commitment to one purpose;

3. the people who form the organisation are motivated by job satisfaction and financial reward for which they are prepared to accept a degree of insecurity;

4. they will be adaptable people and will tend to enlarge their personnel parameters of responsibility up to the point where they are limited by the ambitions of their colleagues.

Type B—Community-centred organisation:

1. Typified by the institutional organisation, it is totally related to the needs of the community, has no need of adaptability, and is wholly committed to one purpose;

2. the people who form the organisation are more motivated by job security for which they are prepared to accept a lower degree of job satisfaction and financial reward;

3. the people tend to be less adaptable and work within narrow, well-determined parameters and schedules of responsibility.

These assumptions resulted from investigation into people's attitudes over a wide range of occupations, including military personnel, hospital workers, teachers, trade unionists, and a wide variety of business people. The work was carried out in 1972 and 1973 and an economic crisis of inflation that has occurred since will have forced changes of attitude. In the present conditions people in type A will be anxious for job security since the opportunity for alternative employment will be limited. People in type B will be as anxious as anyone else for adequate financial reward. But if these modifications to behaviour have been imposed on people by the threat of unemployment and inflation they probably do not change people's fundamental attitudes to their choice of occupation. Business people would still like to be adventurous and nurses would like to be more concerned with patients than pay. The fact that their behaviour has been changed can only result in frustration and an inevitable worsening of industrial relations. In these conditions the task of management is made ever more difficult.

In such conditions of personal, as well as commercial uncertainty, people will tend to become more conscious of a need for job security. Marketing, particularly its sales activities, is not an area renowned for security of occupation. One hopes it will not encourage management to relapse to a "carrot and stick" attitude in its search for control and performance.

It must also be said that while in general, institutions tend to conform to the type B organisational pattern and business firms to type A, there are exceptions to the latter. Many very large business firms, especially those that become king-pins in a local employment situation, tend to conform more to the type B. In those firms, workers tend to be sedentary rather than adventurous and the firms themselves are often forced into a position of being more concerned with existence than profitability.

Span of management

Control and performance evaluation must begin at the top. A manager may delegate his authority for a task but he still retains responsibility. If a subordinate fails to achieve an objective the manager is as responsible for the failure as his subordinate.

No manager can hope to achieve effective control over a span of management that is too wide. The span of management is interconnected with the number of hierarchical levels in an organisation, and this in turn determines the length of the lines of communication. It is a corollary of organisation structures that an increase in the span of management shortens the lines of communication; if the lines of communication are lengthened the span of management is decreased.

It is important that management understands these limitations if it is to control effectively the performance of others. The concepts of a limited span of management are attributed to a number of writers:

General Sir Ian Hamilton recommended: "The average human brain finds its optimum work level when handling three to six other brains." This concept also allows for the span to be greater among first-line supervisors than senior management since the decision-making is likely to be less onerous (*see* Chapter 2, Fig. 8).

Lyndall F. Urwick stressed as a reason for limiting spans of management the recognisable psychological pattern that man has a limited span of attention and therefore is unable to effectively cope with too many problems at once. The sales manager with twelve salesmen reporting directly to him cannot possibly deal with all the problems that they originate.

A. V. Graicunas perceived that it was the complexity of the interactions among the number of subordinates which would ultimately create a breakdown in control. He suggested there is a geometrical progression in the number of interactions which rapidly becomes too large to handle. His theory was built upon the underlying social interactions between a superior and his subordinates.

P. Allen suggested an economic basis of diminishing returns as a reason for limiting the span of management. As extra tasks are added to a manager's responsibilities he is able to perform less effectively and this will cause a gradual diminution of his control.

The importance to marketing of rationalising spans of management lies in the problems of uncontrolled organisational growth.

Some years ago the author was consulted by a firm employing a large number of salesmen selling industrial products. From a successful beginning the firm had grown rapidly and now employed a large number of salesmen. At that time management was concerned that the ratio of calls to orders had fallen significantly and sales costs were rising alarmingly. Analysis of the case suggested the problem originated in too many salesmen reporting to the sales manager.

As the firm had grown, additional salesmen had been employed until the best territories had been occupied and the later salesmen to be appointed had been given the marginal territories. Two points arose from this. The salesmen were operating on territories in which marginal customers required considerably more sales effort to produce results, which was both time consuming and expensive. The second point was that the sales manager had so many salesmen to manage that he could only cope with what he considered to be the most important matters, in this case the more important customers placing large orders. The recommendation to the company was three-fold:

1. To analyse the performance of each territory and cut out those that were too limited in potential ever to be economic.

2. Examine the organisation in total and the performance of individuals with the aim of promoting suitable personnel to be area supervisors in order to reduce the span of management and enable more effective control to be established.

3. Examine the tasks of the sales manager with the aim of delegating work which could be done by subordinates and reduce the volume of reporting to essential items.

Frequently in marketing, personnel are dismissed for poor results when the blame might lie in management's lack of control, guidance and poor communication. The span of management should enable marketing managers to enjoy face-to-face relationships with their immediate subordinates, permit adequate training and guidance to individual personnel on a continuing basis and finally to encourage the optimum in two-way communication to develop.

Marketing controls

Controlling is one of the elements of management along with planning, organising, motivating and co-ordinating. It derives its importance from the need to ensure that the activity of planning is fulfilled in terms of achieving set targets, budgets or schedules.

The role of marketing management in controlling is onerous as many of the targets are dependent upon variables outside its control and based upon forecasts that are themselves only predictions.

Control in marketing should not be solely a matter of governing or directing personnel. Marketing control used in this context also implies verifying and surveying performances.

In marketing, the most important controls are inventory or stock controls, distribution cost analysis, sales control and programme controls.

Management has a prime responsibility for ensuring that work gets done. Personnel will generally do what is necessary for them to do, a minimum performance for which they are employed. Beyond this, however, responsibility for ensuring the work gets done is an involvement with the problem of motivating workers to do more than the compulsory minimum. The problem of attaining a given performance is dependent upon three factors: the persons innate ability to do the job; the degree of training necessary for effective performance; and the conditions of work which make the job irksome.

The result of such inter-relationships will create particular behaviour patterns. The selection of personnel will be a critical factor in the planning function and the fulfilment of company and department objectives. This calls for an understanding of the people who make up the organisation. In this chapter we have already determined that there is a broad distinction to be made between business-centred and community-centred organisations. It is now possible to look at the personnel who elect to work in industry and identify broad differences in them. These are differences arising from background, experience and expectations which have fundamentally affected their attitudes to work and therefore the level of motivation and performance. These differences in attitude may be a criterion for selection and also a means of determining job values. An understanding of the assumptions enables a matching between job and person to take place.

Douglas MacGregor drew up a set of assumptions about the nature of work and of people. These he called Theory X, the work-centred approach, and Theory Y the people-centred approach.

Theory X assumed that work was irksome, unpleasant, an onerous chore to be avoided. It also assumed that to get people to put forward adequate effort they had to be coerced and threatened, that they would avoid work whenever possible and they would avoid all responsibility.

Theory Y assumed that people liked work, that it was as natural for them to expend energy at work as at play, that people enjoyed responsibility and that on the whole in the conditions of modern industrial life they were not stimulated enough mentally.

These are very brief summaries of the main points about theories X and Y, but sufficient for our purpose. Any reader wishing to know more is recommended to the many books on Management Theory and Organisational Behaviour that are available.

From the assumptions it becomes apparent that some people work only for money which is necessary to support themselves and their families. Such people will tend to be job-mobile, they will change their jobs frequently if the prospect of more money is there. Generally these are people who have never had a firm commitment to any one career and therefore to them a job is irksome and an onerous chore. Consider a young person who leaves school as soon as he or she is permitted, to earn money that will enable him to buy records, clothes, etc. Since the objective of work for him is money, it doesn't matter very much what the job is about, building site labourer, warehouse assistant or working in a shop. Without adequate education or training the career prospects are limited. In time the task will become a chore to be avoided as it will lack interest and the person is unlikely to be suitable for promotion. He becomes frustrated and seeks his goals and rewards outside the work situation. So, money becomes the prime mover and the criterion of success.

Professor Frederick Hertzberg suggested a motivation–hygiene theory to explain the attitudes of workers to jobs and money. He suggested there are factors which did not improve the "health" of the worker, but stopped him becoming "unhealthy." His illustration of these hygiene factors was the role of garbage disposal in a city which he explained does not make people healthy, it stops them being unhealthy. Similarly, in the work situation, there are factors which go together to create "hygiene." He saw such hygiene factors as the quality of the supervision, the conditions in which the job is done, the financial rewards and other factors which do not in themselves make workers happy, but stop workers being unhappy. These represent the hygiene factors; what the worker does provides the motivation.

If a worker is given an interesting job, with set and attainable goals providing a standard against which he can measure his own performance, he will be motivated to put forth more than the compulsory minimum. Workers given the opportunity to use initiative and responsibility will be eager to extend this and so achieve more status and authority. This is not to suggest that money is not important, money is the most important hygiene factor and one which Hertzberg termed a replenishment factor: "You eat now, you've got to eat again later." But it does not provide the sole drive for effort and only serves to stop workers becoming unhappy for financial reasons.

As a technique for evaluating performance, motivation is very important. No amount of controls will persuade workers to do more than they have to. The way all too many salesmen are controlled illustrates the worst aspects of a disciplinary, work-centred approach.

The salesman is given a basic salary, the rest of his income he has to earn by means of commission on sales. He has to account for his time, often in considerable detail, and frequently has little involvement with the firm in terms of planning or co-ordination. Under such conditions it is no wonder salesmen tend to be highly mobile. Managers who ask their sales force to account for every moment of their time and are suspicious that their men are taking time off, or doing something on the side, coerce them further, introduce more controls, trust them less and are surprised when they find their men behaving true to form, a self-fulfilling prophecy.

To ensure performance and, most important, a responsible, imaginative and well-motivated sales force, or any other personnel, they must be selected with an understanding of the needs of the job, trained adequately and on a continuous basis, paid at a level to remove the "unhappiness" factor, given sufficient status and clear and attainable objectives.

It is important that marketing management should accept that traditional views regarding the "carrot and stick" attitude are not helpful in the modern social climate. On the whole people are much better educated and informed than ever before and it seems strange that such people are often trained to do less and less. The following points are taken from *Sales and Sales Management* and suggest a new way of approach to the job:

1. Work is an indispensable part of a person's life and is the part which gives status and links with the community.

2. Generally men like their work and those instances when they do not are attributable to the conditions of the job in terms of the prevailing psychological and social attitudes in the firm.

3. The workers' morale has no positive relationship to the physical conditions of the job. Although poor physical conditions may have an effect upon the workers' health and well-being, they have no influence on morale.

4. Under normal conditions money is the least important incentive. The greatest negative incentive is the fear of unemployment because it removes the worker from his particular society.

Analysis of cost and performance

Distribution cost analysis is a system of allocating expenditure according to the use to which it is put. Through the use of distribution cost analysis, marketing management is able to institute a control by comparing actual with standard performance with the objective of ensuring that a small number of products, or customers, do not account for a disproportionately large part of total sales or profits.

On the sales side too great a reliance upon a small number of customers is a dangerous situation for the company and the individual salesman since a relatively small change in the market can result in a major loss of sales revenue.

To give an example of this situation, a company selling corrosion-resistant coatings had a salesman in the Birmingham area, which being at the centre of the metal finishing industry in Britain, provided a large number of customers.

In 1967 the Ministry of Defence introduced a new standard of finish for naval rescue beacons and most of the work was undertaken by a metal finisher in the Birmingham area. During the three month period the salesman devoted nearly all his time to this account and neglected many of his former accounts and a significant amount of business was lost to competitors. The salesman's monthly reports however were inflated by his sales to the metal finisher and during this period his sales exceeded his targets to the satisfaction of the sales manager. It was only when the defence contract finished that the true state was revealed, for during this short period they had accounted for more than 80 per cent of his sales, and on their ceasing his sales slumped, revealing how his neglect of former customers had lost their business.

Fig. 40 is a Lorenz curve which represents graphically the kind of situation described.

It does not have to be a salesman and his customers which create this position. A firm of casting manufacturers developed an export market for one type of product which was so successful that other less successful products were dropped and resources reallocated to produce the big seller. Then with little warning the market collapsed under two pressures—the appearance of a new type of product which superseded the casting and a change in economic conditions which brought about the decline of the export market.

Distribution cost accounting allocates expenditure incurred in accomplishing the marketing objectives to the activities employed, *i.e.* advertising, selling, transportation, packaging, etc. Expenses are allocated to the centre incurring it, whether a product, customer, market segment or person. Four kinds of analysis may be considered:

1. Internal cost analysis.
2. Marketing activities analysis.

3. Segmented cost analysis.
4. Marginal contribution analysis.

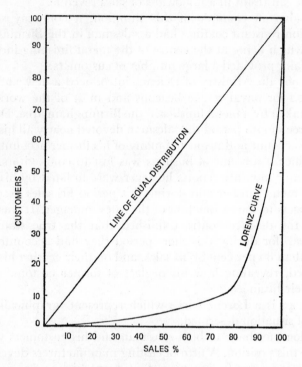

FIG. 40.—*Lorenz curve.*

Internal cost analysis

Accountancy practice recognises that certain costs are entirely internal to the operations of the business; they are sometimes referred to as natural expenses. Examples of internal costs are salaries, wages, taxes, telephone and postal charges, material costs, etc.

All these internal charges may be allocated against the various activities of marketing. Certain costs such as telephone calls, petrol consumption and luncheon vouchers may be attributed to the sales force. Other costs may be attributed to transportation, warehousing, credit control or some other activity within the marketing function.

Internal costs analysis breaks down allocated costs and compares them between different branches, territories or activities over a predetermined time period. A problem arises out of using internal costs as a means of control since there can be no definable objective in terms of what measurable standard ought to be used. A measure of control is achieved from the process of comparison between the different sales personnel, products, territories and so on. Even then it is difficult to assess an individual's performance in terms of costs for which the individual may have little responsibility.

Internal costs rarely meet this criterion of being within the sphere of an individual's control. It is still possible, however, for a firm to obtain an assessment of the benefits of its internal costs by the use of industry-based cost ratios from which it can take guidance as to its situation relative to comparable firms.

Marketing activities analysis

Marketing activities analysis aims to establish a basis of control over expenditure associated with the activities applied to sales, products, marketing research, promotions, etc.

It begins with the identification of activities for which marketing is responsible and establishes operations on a functional basis to include all those activities, as described in Chapter 2. Following this, any internal costs are classified in functional groupings to reveal which costs are attributable to marketing activities.

The next step is to determine some rational basis for allocating variable costs to each functional group. Once this has been done, the total cost for each marketing activity, e.g. the sales force, can be established and all activities aggregated to produce a total marketing functional cost. It now provides a further basis for comparison over a time period such as a yearly budgeting period. It can be used as a basis for assessing the cost effectiveness of different activities within the marketing function and affords a means of establishing how much each activity is worth as a part of the functional effort and whether it can be improved.

Segmented cost analysis

Extending marketing activities analysis a stage further enables control to be applied to product ranges, sales territories and customer groups. The efficient performance of marketing management necessitates surveillance of managerial responsibilities and segmented cost analysis enables a control element to be introduced.

Segmented cost analysis examines how costs are applied to various problems arising out of the marketing activities and whether this expenditure results in measurable benefits. Marketing losses generally result from products failing to reach their break-even point, or distribution costs being unexpectedly high perhaps because products fail to reach a predicted level of demand. Poor sales force training will result in badly organised territories incurring high expenses in travelling and also an unacceptably high cost per customer.

Just as organisation structures can be analysed by a process of departmentation, so the marketing operation can be analysed through a concept of segments. Segments are parts cut off or separable from other parts of something. In marketing, segmentation enables a distinction to be made between identifiable parts of the total process; this may be by product, customer, or marketing/sales strategy.

Product segmentation will include brands, types of product or commodities. Customers can be segmented according to geography, size of annual purchases, order size, type of purchases and delivery methods. Marketing/sales strategy can be according to the channels of distribution, sales methods or on the basis of pricing and discount structure.

The following case is an example. Company A, an electrical wholesaler, segmented customers according to their annual purchases and allocated marketing costs to each segment. From the total number of accounts, spread over a large area of South Wales and the West Country, 36 per cent accounted for only 9 per cent of total company sales. By a continuing process of cost analysis and sales control the unprofitable customers were dropped and the company concentrated on customers able to provide orders of an economic size. During a period of three years sales increased by 73 per cent while marketing costs were reduced from 26 per cent of sales to 14 per cent resulting in a net profit of 12 per cent whereas before the analytical process had been carried out the company had a loss of 3 per cent of sales. The problems of sales control will be discussed more fully in Chapter 10, but here it is sufficient to appreciate how a technique of analysis can produce positive results.

Marginal contribution analysis

Marginal contribution analysis is an alternative to the less exact application of full cost allocation. Full cost analysis which arbitrarily allocates common costs that cannot be positively attributed to a specific marketing activity, offer little scope for a basis of control.

Marginal contribution analysis entails assessing only those costs which are incurred as a direct result of servicing particular customers or selling particular products. Analysis is concerned only with costs that could be saved by dropping a product or customer. In full cost allocation dropping an unprofitable product simply means re-allocating the costs among the remaining products and not infrequently this added burden on a marginally profitable product turns it into an unprofitable product; the domino theory of product profitability will be discussed further in Chapter 8.

For decisions on whether to add or drop a product, marginal contribution analysis provides the most relevant information because it is relative profitability of customer segments, product ranges or selling methods that is important. Following an analysis into the marginal costs, it may be decided to retain a low or marginally profitable product and investigate further into the causes of low profitability. Correctly applied it is a powerful means of providing data for marketing decision-making.

CHAPTER EIGHT

Product strategy and planning

Product policy

All companies have to take decisions on the range of products they will produce. Like all management decisions, product decisions will operate within the framework of the company's policy laid down by the Board of Directors. This policy, interpreted by the Managing Director, will be delegated to the functional heads for implementation.

Although both production and marketing have a major responsibility for product policy, the manner in which the Board deals with interconnected policy questions will have a greater effect on the company's overall success than cost reduction activities at management level.

Implementation of product policy falls within the responsibility of both production and marketing functions. Both will contribute to the eventual shape of the product range by imposing constraints and by suggesting innovations. The kind of constraints are likely to be limitations of what can be produced in terms of production, and what will be acceptable to customers in terms of marketing. Innovations on the production side arise by improved materials, components or methods of making, while the marketing side will report back new trends and competitors' developments.

Product policy decisions include:

1. The number of products the company offers;
2. what sort of products they should be;
3. the timing of new product introduction and the form it should take;
4. the effect that introduction of new products will have on the existing range and whether some of the older products should be re-designed or discontinued.

Marketing has greatly accelerated the pace at which products change. During the last twenty years in Britain, and rather longer in the United States, marketing has kept consumers buying by a process of innovation giving consumers reasons, however trivial they may seem, to replace products. An example of this is the development of the washing machine market.

Originally the washing machine was a fairly simple "tub" with an agitator. The product then went through stages of development; first a heater was added, then a pump, then a wringer, followed by a power wringer. The spin dryer was at first a complementary product but soon became integrated into a "twin-tub" machine. The final product, to date, is the automatic machine. But what will be next to induce housewives to change their present machines for other, later models?

A similar example has been the television receiver. When the market for black-and-white receivers was virtually saturated, the introduction of BBC 2 on 625 lines made all existing receivers obsolete and opened a new market. Now the introduction of colour has created a third market. This process of product change is shown in the form of a replacement cycle in Fig. 41.

Today there are few companies that can be confident that a

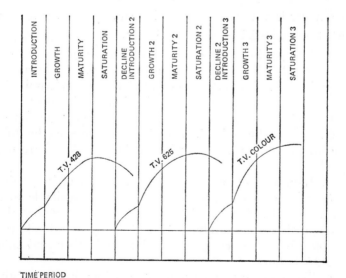

FIG. 41.—*Replacement cycle.*

good product, or range of products, will last for a period of years. Marketing, as we have seen, has accelerated the rate of change but other pressures have contributed to this rapid change rate, *e.g.* the pace of technological development and introduction of new processes. There are numerous examples of the impact on manufacturers of developments of these kinds:

1. Introduction of paper-back books;
2. artificial fibres;
3. printed and photographed circuits;
4. new wrapping materials;
5. substitution of plastic for metal in manufacture of rain-water pipes and brackets.

The problem is not that firms are unaware that these changes are occurring and are oblivious to their effects, but that too few companies rationally plan for them or adapt their product range to take advantage. Unfortunately British industry has never seemed to realise the importance of making the product match the market, in spite of a long history of inventiveness and technical ability.

Strategies and objectives of planning

A company is able to adapt varying strategies without going outside its existing product range:

1. By a profit-maximisation strategy implemented through a rigorously planned cost reduction campaign. There is a built-in constraint to this, however, since profit maximisation may be achieved through reduction in spending on promotion, packaging, development or other aspects of the marketing-mix variables. An increased profit achieved by these means this year may result in a falling market share next year.

2. It may undertake optimisation studies of its product mix in an endeavour to reduce the range available to its customers. In doing so the company must acknowledge, though, that some products which may be marginally profitable do attract customers to buy the other and more profitable lines.

3. The company can extend its markets for the existing range by developing its existing sales outlets and reputation

and so encourage greater consumption. Or it may adapt its present products so that they appeal more widely. An example of this is the advent of the tea bag as an approach to the problem of competing with instant coffee.

4. It can extend its facilities for producing existing products either by expanding existing plant or by purchasing other companies. Skol International lager resulted from the needs of a medium-sized brewery to expand its sales and reputation internationally. The strategy was achieved by a group of medium-sized breweries in several countries agreeing to produce and market an identical lager that would permit them to compete internationally with the very largest breweries. If a company can also add new products to its range or enter new markets, then additional strategies become possible.

5. The company may undertake sub-contract work, exemplified by the clothing firms which produce for Marks & Spencer Ltd. In this way major new products can be manufactured without the problems of locating a market, or taking undue risk on innovation.

6. It may undertake to manufacture under licence. The Carmen Hair Curler Company make hairdryers under licence from the Schick Corporation of the United States. This is the reverse of the last strategy, since here the company has a marketing task rather than a production one.

7. A company may purchase other companies and integrate their production and marketing activities. This frequently happens in the food industry. The Avana Bakery Group now controls many formerly independent pie-makers which now market their products under the common brand name of "Fleur de lys." The group also controls manufacturers of preserves and jams which are used in the production of their range of cakes, many of which are produced for Marks & Spencer Ltd.

8. Finally a company may develop new products for existing or for new markets, the latter representing the most risky form of innovation since the company is taking risks on both production and marketing. Generally however, a company develops markets or products which make use of existing expertise. For example, the industrial paint company which, using its knowledge of solvents and its awareness of industrial degreasing problems put the two together and

formulated a range of industrial degreasers which it marketed to large caterers and hotels. This was an entirely new product for a completely new market.

There is a danger in diversifying too far, especially if it leads a company to offer too large a variety of products. Figs. 42 and

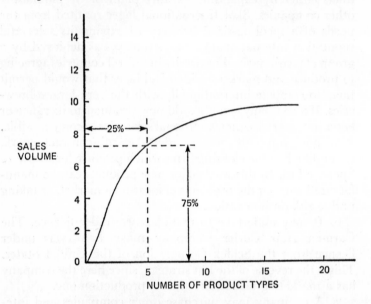

FIG. 42.—*Distribution of sales by product.*

43 show the effect on costs of such a company in which 25 per cent of the product range accounts for 75 per cent of sales volume. Frequently this situation means that a small part of the range earns the greater part of the profit, while many products are making a loss. As we shall see below, it may be acceptable that certain products sell below cost so long as in doing so they encourage the buying of the profitable lines, and so long as it is not a permanent feature.

Generally the reason why this situation arises is that over the years new products have been added to the range but the old products have not been dropped. No logical attempt has been made to restrict the range with the objective of increased profitability. This is not an uncommon situation for an adventurous marketing-oriented company to find itself in.

A company successfully manufactures and sells a range of

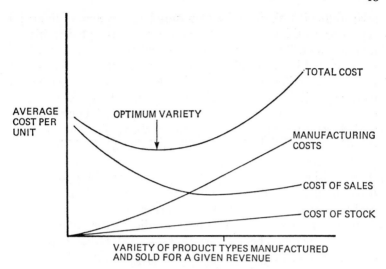

FIG. 43.—*Optimum variety of product range.*

products, and in time customers ask for variations or modifications. These are introduced and lead to increased sales and so more are added. In times of economic growth this is a fair practice since all companies are buoyant and confident and the variations lead to further segmentation of the market and are necessary to counter competitors' activity. At some time, however, the company finds that the cost of maintaining this range has resulted in a falling profitability. The company is then faced with a major task of reducing the range due to the size of the problem arising from it.

Case Study

An example of this situation is a manufacturer of electrical components. This company had been established some twenty-five years, had national sales, a good reputation and good products. Too many years of poor management, however, had resulted in falling profits, increased pressure from competitors and a weak management structure which had arisen from the lack of directive from the top. This in turn had been aggravated by a policy of internal promotion only.

Consultants were asked to look into the reasons for the falling profitability and see if there was any potential for expansion.

Initially the consultants set about collecting information, itself a difficult task since the firm only had a system of financial reporting as this was the only information presented to higher management. The consultants collected the data on trends of sales, available by examining past invoices, prices and discount structures, to show product profitability. The existing cost data were not reliable because the overheads, a large part of total cost, were calculated on the content of direct labour and this varied considerably according to product. The unreliability therefore cast serious doubts on the existing profitability.

The company manufactured 2,500 standard items, each in three finishes and six sizes, which gave a total of 45,000 items listed in their catalogues. This was far in excess of anything realised by management. It was necessary to calculate sales volume for each product and to eradicate the items of low volume since it had been shown that slightly less that 20 per cent of the product range accounted for 95 per cent of total sales. Once this had been done the range was reduced to a manageable size of 9,000 standard items.

The reduced range was now critically examined by the introduction of cost-centred costing with the aim of obtaining a more exact cost of each product and its profitability, which would enable the introduction of a more realistic pricing structure and system of discounts. This would permit development of a sensible product development policy. A system of management control was introduced so that information would be communicated to management and enable it to direct the company effectively. As a result of the investigation two benefits were obtained:

1. Variety reduction reduced costs:
    (a) Manufacturing costs were reduced through longer production runs, increased throughput and a reduction of the labour force;
    (b) inventory costs were reduced as the range of products was reduced;
    (c) administrative costs of selling, invoicing and accounting were reduced.

2. Future planning became possible once the confusion of too many products was removed:
    (a) Market research information was related to true cost and profit data;

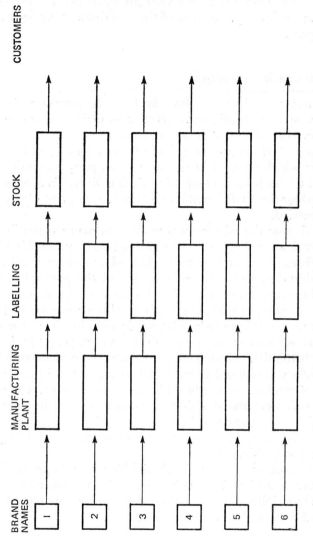

BRAND NAMES

MANUFACTURING PLANT

LABELLING

STOCK

CUSTOMERS

1

2

3

4

5

6

FIG. 44.—Manufacture, stock and distribution before variety reduction.

(b) it became possible to undertake marketing and product planning;

(c) it was possible to investigate the benefits of low cost/ high volume production of the remaining, much-reduced range.

Product rationalisation

The variety problem can also arise from the purchase of competitors and the continued marketing of their products under their own brand names for sales reasons.

A large food manufacturer had taken over many of its competitors which resulted in the parent company marketing six different brands each comprising similar lines. To service the demand for the six different brand distributions, 1,000 lines had to be carried.

In this case the solution was to align as many as possible of the specifications between the brands so that they were identical apart from the name and packaging. Manufacture could then be undertaken for a common stock and the packaging and branding completed for bulk batches drawn from the common stock according to sales. Once this had been accomplished the company was able to reduce branded stocks in the warehouse. This process is shown diagrammatically in Figs. 44 and 45. It also meant better deliveries to customers since the problem of replacing stocks was reduced to one of labelling. In this instance the range of products was reduced by some 60 per cent, while the volume of orders placed with production to replace the common stock fell by 50 per cent although production runs were much longer and allowed considerable cost economies leading to greater competitiveness.

It is important to emphasise the significant rise in profitability that may be achieved through rationalising the product range. This is especially so in a situation where a company has a large range of items with low profitability.

1. If products sell in small quantities and have to be made in small batches it results in excessive downtime and a corresponding increase in overheads.

2. Products which sell in small quantities frequently require special raw material stocks, tools and equipment all

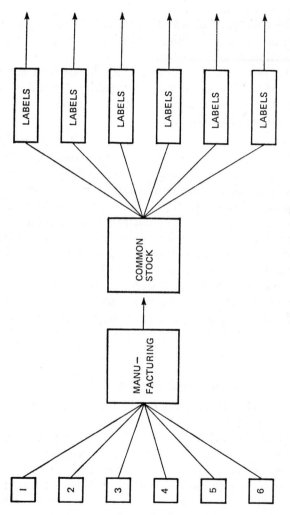

Fig. 45.—*Aligned specifications.*

of which demand extra space and capital, which could possibly be put to better use.

3. Finished goods also require warehousing and may present an additional problem if extensive stocks of spares have to be carried.

4. The selling and distribution effort is frequently an extra demand on sales, advertising and distribution, leading to a disproportionate cost burden.

5. The products will present extra burdens in terms of design and production as well as requiring the full complement of records to be kept on costings, statistics and work measurements of all kinds.

How far does a company go in applying product rationalising schemes? Certainly there are few limits to a company reducing the variety of its products but the firm's ability to rationalise customers is limited. A company that significantly reduces its range of products may also find it has caused a reduction in its range of customers, unless it can attract new customers for its reduced range. Effective variety reduction frequently leads to reductions in costs which may be passed on to customers in the form of lower prices, which in turn can lead to increased sales volume from the remaining customers. Where the price is a relatively unimportant consideration to the customer in his choice of purchases, some lost sales may result from variety reduction. This will also occur if a customer prefers to buy all his requirements from one supplier.

Variety reduction in product planning

The initial step in planning the product range it to examine the needs of the market, both at home and abroad. It is important that the economies which are to be gained by a process of variety reduction are related to the effects on sales volume and income and the level of profitability. The objective is to determine a range of products with the least possible variety of raw materials and components but which will nevertheless provide sufficient variety for the company to sustain its position in the market (*see* Fig. 46). To rationalise the product range requires the company to obtain much information, which may be difficult to obtain, but without it a logical process of product planning and a marketing policy is impossible.

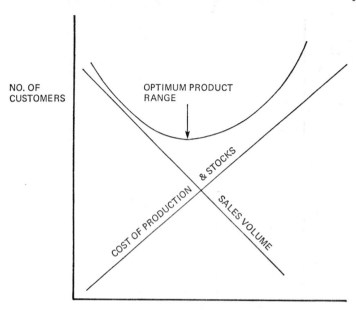

NO. OF
CUSTOMERS

OPTIMUM PRODUCT
RANGE

& STOCKS

COST OF PRODUCTION

SALES VOLUME

NO. OF END — PRODUCTS

Fig. 46.—*Optimum product range.*

It is necessary to obtain information on sales volume for each product or type of product. This is then analysed in terms of the parameters relevant to that product. Fig. 47 illustrates a way the analysis may be undertaken, and should result in showing which products are apparently in demand. It would still be necessary to investigate further to clarify the reasons for market preferences; these may be price, size, reliability, performance or technical achievement. Also, of course, volume of sales is not the sole criterion by which decisions can be taken.

Any product range study must also examine profitability as well as sales volume. Analysis of any range of products will show some products selling well and others badly and frequently a wide variation between profit and loss. Fig. 48 illustrates such an analysis, but it is not often that product policy can be determined from so simple an analysis. The problem is that while it might appear at first sight logical to discontinue loss-incurring products in order to maximise profits, this ignores the contribution to overheads made by the loss products. If the recovery

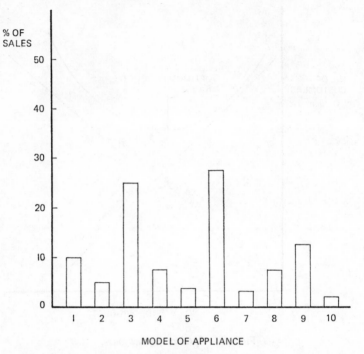

FIG. 47.—*Distribution of sales.*

of overheads had to be from profitable products only, it might convert the profits on the products into an overall loss.

Before any product is discarded there are a number of questions to ask about why certain products make a loss:

1. Wrong price? How does it compare with competitors' product prices?

2. Too high costs? Is it possible to correct the cost structure?

In answering these questions the firm must ascertain that the cost and profit data are themselves accurate, since any costing method cannot be more than an approximation of the truth. However the firm goes about collecting such information it will have to strike a balance between the cost involved and the accuracy required.

The allocation of some production overheads between pro-

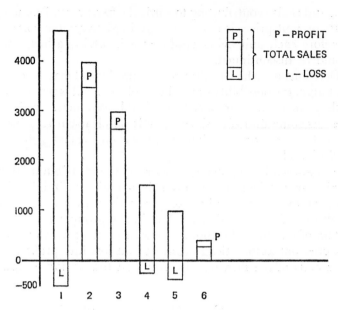

Fig. 48.—*Profitability of product types.*

ducts may be apportioned with accuracy while others may have to be allocated on a rule of thumb basis. Among the latter will be the space occupied—how much of the factory space does a product take up in being made, one third, a half?; the process times measured in man-hours; and the total cost of the product or the costs of inspection and quality control.

Some products may be unfairly loaded and so distort the assessment of profitability among the product range. Works management must find the appropriate costing method which will enable, at the lowest cost of collection, the most accurate method of apportioning these costs among the product range. Any assessment of product policy can only be made after it has been ascertained that the cost and profit data are reasonably accurate.

Given that the cost and profit data are reasonably accurate it is then possible to examine product policy on a basis of marginal costing. Fig. 49 illustrates three products in different situations.

Product A is in a profitable situation in which both its variable cost and fixed cost are covered by the price. Product B is covering its variable costs of raw materials, labour, electricity,

F

etc., and is also contributing towards the fixed costs. Product C, at its present price, is not even covering its variable costs and therefore each unit being produced is incurring a loss, and it should be discontinued.

Decisions on when to discontinue product C may be dependent upon the possibility or need to replace it, if it is popular and perhaps attracts customers to profitable products. Product B presents some difficulty since there is no clear-cut solution on its replacement or retention unless one undertakes a different kind of analysis.

As was seen in Chapter 1, in assessing the contribution that a particular product makes towards overall profitability it is relevant to consider only those costs that are incurred as a result of maintaining that product in the product range. In a system of full cost allocation, to drop a product which shows a loss does not automatically convert that loss into profit as the fixed costs of the firm remain. Any cost that is non-escapable

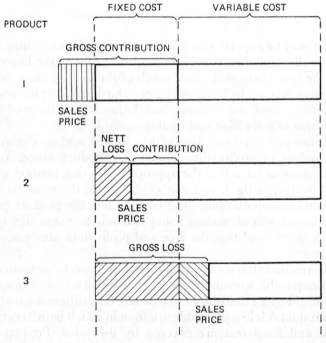

FIG. 49.—*Marginal costing.*

will then have to be re-allocated among other products. In marginal contribution analysis costs that can be re-allocated to other products are not considered. This precludes management from getting rid of a product which is adding more to revenue than to costs despite its inability to bear its full burden of indirect costs. Therefore a decision to drop product B must be considered in terms of marginal contribution analysis which provides the essential information for this type of decision.

Marketing management in particular is faced with decisions if the price cannot be increased, nor costs reduced and assuming the data are accurate. It must now seek justification for retaining such a product. Will it affect customer loyalty? How will its removal affect the present comprehensive range? What effect does selling this product have on other product sales?

If marketing wishes to retain the product, how much will the decision cost in terms of lost profit and how necessary is it to introduce a new product on a profitable basis? What will be the cost of the introduction?

If it is decided that from a marketing viewpoint it is unnecessary to retain the product it raises further questions. How can the spare production capacity be more profitably utilised and what other products are likely to provide the extra volume? If there are positive answers to these questions then marketing will proceed on those assumptions, but if it is not certain that the capacity can be utilised at a profit, can the spare capacity be disposed of? This might be achieved by selling off the unwanted plant or by letting a part of the factory.

Liquidating assets is not always easy, and at the time of writing, those firms with spare capacity would find great difficulty in acquiring a taker. Some overheads are in any case integral and cannot be disposed of piecemeal. In these circumstances the unemployed capacity would continue as overheads that would have to be distributed among the remaining products and could then adversely affect their profitability.

In the business situation all decisions have far-reaching effects and in practice product decisions cannot be made in isolation. The dropping of one product will affect the potential profitability of another, a domino theory of product profitability in which the fall of one is likely to bring down its fellows in turn. Any decision on one product has to be seen in relation to the remainder of the range. In most cases firms do not know what effect such a move will have and must seek further information. In such a situation of uncertainty operational research techniques can help in providing answers to complex operational problems.

Applying operational research

We have seen in Chapter 4 how operational research can be applied to the marketing problem. In relation to the problems of product policy, it is worth bearing in mind that operational research is by its nature a protracted method of analysis. In applying O.R. the researcher will examine the particular problem and then use an appropriate method of analysis to seek the solution. An organisation which finds it needs an answer to its problems tomorrow has not devoted sufficient preparation to the questions of tomorrow. If a firm finds itself in need of an "instant" product policy decision it will find that O.R. cannot provide on that time scale.

Given accurate cost and profit data O.R. can apply techniques of linear programming to determine the optimum product-mix in terms of profitability. But marketing management's optimum mix may not be the same as production management's optimum mix. If the linear programming is commissioned by marketing management there will be a tendency for the programme to be fed data that accounts well for its own activity but does not adequately represent the activities of other functions, such as production. An optimum mix expressed in terms of profits and prices with marketing constraints may present production with a nonsense. Of course the opposite may apply. Production losses and unnecessary costs, inadequate exploitation of the market and unnecessarily low profits may result from minimal differences in production and facilities.

Policy considerations may also impose limitations on an optimum solution. Marketing factors such as those already determined may result in a policy objection to discontinuing products. There are also social considerations if shutting a particular factory results in increased unemployment in the community. Industrial relations or government policy may also conflict with the company's policy.

Operational research cannot produce an answer to all these problems, but the application of linear programming can show the cost of policy decisions by determining the differences between the optimum solution and the best solution that is available and within the company's policy.

In a product policy problem involving the utilisation of capacity the degree of complexity arising from the need to provide a solution will depend on how many products are involved and what are the constraints. In a situation where only four products are involved and there is a single capacity constraint the problem is relatively simple. The output of the most profitable product is maximised first, and then the output of the second one and so on. Where a firm has a large number of products with a whole range of inter-relating constraints then the problem may be too complex and its solution needs a computer.

Once the cost and profit data have been collected the computer operation may be a relatively quick process and not expensive. It is in the collection of the information that the costs are heavy and the use of O.R. in a situation where no relevant information has previously been collected may be lengthy. Generally, however, companies would justify the expenditure by the improvement in control that results.

An example of improved control allowing better profits is to be found in those shipyards undertaking government contracts. In the early 1960s the Ferranti company was producing electronic and missile equipment under government contracts. Later the government claimed Ferranti had made excessive profits which in due course the company had to repay. Following that affair, any major government contractor had to have very accurate records of costs. In the shipyards in particular it resulted in the government contractors maintaining profitability at a time when other yards were incurring losses.

Economic appraisal of product policy

In appraising its product policy, the company's objective is to ensure profitability and its success is measured in these terms. Its task is two-fold:

    1. Comparison between existing products; and
    2. appraisal of new products.

Comparison between existing products is concerned with the control of product policy and it is necessary to ensure a continuous feedback of product profitability information, as shown in Table XIV.

TABLE XIV. *Product profitability*. This information, collected in table form for each product, is extended to a total.

Items	Product range					Total
	1	2	3	4	5	
1. Costs						
labour						
materials						
2. Overheads						
specific to product						
general						
3. Total sales cost						
profit						
sales income						
4. % profit on costs						
5. Capital employed at						
historical cost						
% profit on capital employed						
6. Capital employed at						
replacement costs						
% profit on capital employed						

It will be one of the main functions of the Board to preserve and improve the profitability of the capital employed. To show how the capital invested in the past relates to earnings in the present the percentage profit on the capital employed at historical cost is included. To provide an equitable basis for comparison with current new products, the percentage profit on capital employed at a replacement cost is also included.

While in principle such an analysis is fairly simple, in practice management encounters a number of factors upon which arbitrary assumptions must be made. These include the allocation of overheads between products, the choice of depreciation rates and how research and development costs are to be allocated. These may be treated as a capital item forming part of the investment, or treated as an overhead which may or may not be allocated to a specific product and set against sales revenue in each accounting period.

Such a process of analysis provides the basic data from which management decisions can be taken on questions of product policy. From the analysis the Board is informed of which products have been most successful and have produced the most satisfying return on the original investment.

In its appraisal of new products, the company examines each new product and compares it with existing products in its range to determine whether a prescribed level of sales and profit have been met and to see what influence the new product has had on the company's overall position. Some new products may not only be best sellers in themselves but can have a decisive and beneficial effect on other products in the range, especially complementary ones. A paint company introduced a new plastic coating in 1966. It was an immediate success but also boosted sales of a primer that the company had been selling in small quantities for many years. Firms who had hitherto not bought the primer found it excellent and within a short while it was selling independently of the new product and on its own merits. Of course, all too often a new product has an adverse effect. Consumers in particular are not very loyal and a bad product soon rubs off on others in the range even if they had been previously well thought of.

A product appraisal is made for a number of years. Starting with the launch date it shows what has been invested in the product and the resulting profits. Fig. 50 relates this information to the product's life-cycle and it will be seen that eventually the accumulated profits catch up with accumulated investment at a pay-off date. While most new products will need a heavy investment early in the cycle, it is hoped that this will tail off after its acceptance and the return will then exceed the investment. One of the major problems in this analysis though is to know what costs are being incurred.

Any successful product attracts competition and after a while the selling and distribution costs begin to rise, but may not be noticed or easily measured. If competition becomes severe the company may have to launch further promotional campaigns or even invest further in redesigned packaging. All too many products, which have been costed with reasonable accuracy in production and launch, lose their way in the battle for sales when their unprofitability may be hidden charges against the sales effort and company as a whole.

A Profit and Loss Account for the new product will on the

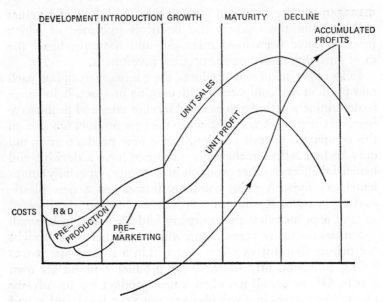

FIG. 50.—*Life-cycle and profitability.*

expenditure side include the product's variable costs and the overheads allocated to the product. It will in addition include the product's launching costs amortised for a fixed number of years and treated as an expenditure item. The expenditures are offset against the expected sales income and will produce a Profit and Loss Account to be related to the level of investment and show the product's anticipated profitability.

Such an analysis can be used to produce an estimated pay-off date. Fig. 51 illustrates the construction of such a graph. The investment increases during the early stages of the product— research and development costs, pre-marketing and production costs, the launch costs and the extra investment to promote the product in its early life. When the product is on sale the profitability will gradually increase as sales build up. Since the investment will at some point tail off, the profitability will exceed it at some time. The amount of financing needed at any time will be the vertical distance between the profit curve and the investment curve. The duration of the unprofitable period will be the horizontal distance between the initial investment and the pay-off date.

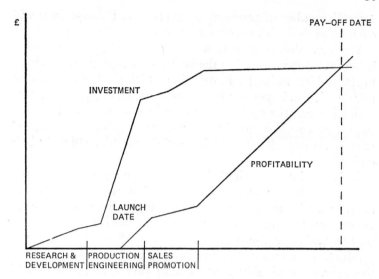

Fig. 51.—*Launch and pay-off date.*

The actual profitability will not begin until the product starts to sell and will begin to accumulate before the investment is completed. When sales reach a regular volume the investment will have been completed and the profitability will be established at a steady level.

Any such analysis must be based on an estimate of costs, and the volume of sales over a period of time. The length of time allowed for amortisation of the launching costs will have an important effect on the profitability of the company and the new venture in particular. Generally the period will be based on the company's financial position, but the expected life of the product will be a major constraint. If the anticipated life of the product is five years then obviously it is pointless to plan to recover the costs over a longer period.

Selecting new products

For the products that have originated in the market survey the analysis discussed above will be undertaken and the feasibility of each one considered. It is unlikely, however, that the company will have the resources, research, material or finance to produce all the new ideas, so the next step is the selection of a small number of products by a process of comparison with each other and with current products.

We have already seen that the estimated life of the product is important in calculating the write-off period in the product's profit and loss estimate. In deciding which products to produce this date is also important in determining the likely pay-off date, which is when the company will get its money back. The more important consideration however is the length of the product's life *after* the pay-off date and the level the product will make in its entire life.

It is possible to calculate for each product an estimated average profit per year of its life. This average profit is then compared with the investment to produce a figure representing average profitability per year. Each product is then compared on this basis and the highest average profitability product or products are selected. Further comparisons can be made with the average profitability of existing products and also with the desired level of profitability which will be a parameter of product selection.

Like all methods of market analysis it has its faults and while presenting a basis for comparison and selection it does leave other problems unanswered.

A new product will rarely duplicate existing products in terms of production, research or marketing facilities and unless entirely new facilities are created, the company is faced with a change in the structure of the existing product-mix. This must then lead to further examinations of production capacity and volume, allocation of overheads and their recovery and the optimum utilisation of the resources generally.

Companies also differ in their financial ability. If a company is short of cash or experiences difficulty in raising finance on acceptable terms, it will have a quite different attitude to product development than a company with adequate financial ability. A company may have to liquidate assets which will leave it with a large sum of money available for further investment. If it cannot find an external investment offering better return than that to be had by investing internally in a new product then it will go ahead with such a product development. The whole complexity of and the interreactions in the process of product selection are shown in model form in Fig. 52.

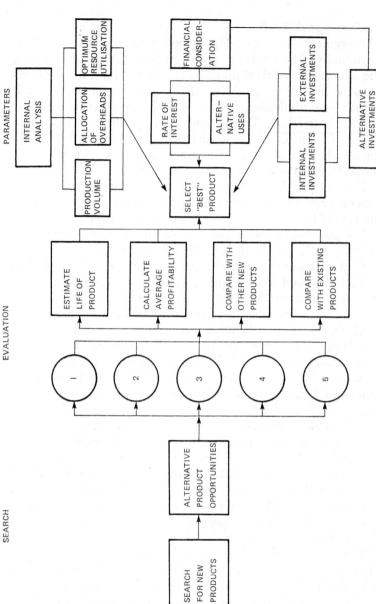

SEARCH   EVALUATION   PARAMETERS

FIG. 52.—*Selection and evaluation of products.*

Continuous product policy

Management needs to adopt a policy of reviewing products continually. The needs of consumers will undergo change and the appearance of rival products creates the need for the company to modify its products. If management postpones such decisions until declining sales force it upon them, then the change is too late. To introduce new products is a lengthy process if failures are to be avoided. This fear of failure frequently leads management to constant review of products in the hope that the next one might be better.

Product decisions are an activity of management planning that occur at an increasing pace. In the recent past a good product could have lasted perhaps fifteen or even twenty years with only slight modification. Indeed some products are still selling after a very long time during which they have undergone no, or very slight, changes, *e.g.* Guinness, Horlicks, Ovaltine and Oxo.

Technical and marketing innovations now occur at an ever-increasing rate of change and five years may be the average product life, although in the field of electronics and pharmaceuticals six months may be more accurate.

It is often said, especially by overseas customers, that Britain is slow to change and tends to cling to outdated products and methods of production. In the past this may well have been true and largely resulted from Britain's dependence upon traditional "Empire" markets which provided an environment in which the strongest competition was largely excluded by means of preferential tariffs and conventional buying practices. The sudden elimination of these markets and the resulting competition exposed this fundamental weakness of British business practice with calamitous results. The protected market bred complacency which failed to provide the most modern production methods that our main competitors, Germany, United States, Japan and France, had invested in.

The product life-cycle illustrated in Fig. 50 shows the phases of development—introduction, growth, maturity and decline. The time period of each phase of the cycle will vary according to the product. Rapidly moving consumer products may have a pattern which will be a regular movement and enable a replacement product to be introduced with a fairly accurate predictability. Industrial products however, may have very irregular patterns over long periods. Product replacement in the industrial field is often a case of changing technology. The steam boiler, after a twenty-year life, is replaced by an entirely different source of energy altogether. In practical terms a company cannot permit a product to go too far into decline before it takes action. Fig. 53 shows that a product which is going into the decline phase may actually have been experiencing falling profitability for some time. The fall in unit profit is the result of the company being forced to compete in areas other than price. If competition is severe the company may have to

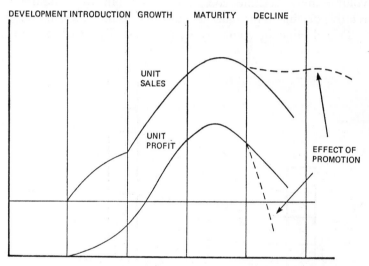

FIG. 53.—*Product life-cycle and promotion.*

increase its delivery schedules to include less economic loads, undertake special variations or even increase the number of sales calls per volume of orders. None of these charges are readily allocatable to the product but they are being spent.

What happens if the company decides to increase promotional activity to increase demand for a flagging product? The broken lines of Fig. 53 indicate that although the promotion may increase sales it only does so at increased cost, a very practical example of the effects of diminishing marginal returns.

If the company decides to replace the declining product then at what stage is this to be done? To introduce the replacement too soon may kill a product that was only suffering a temporary decline and would have recovered. To introduce it too late may mean that the customers will have switched to other brands and may be very difficult to win back without a costly promotional campaign. This often leads to the replacement product not achieving a sufficient share of the market and, in turn, its replacement achieves less again. In this way a declining market share results as each replacement product hits its peak sales below the peak of the preceding product.

If a market is expanding in its total size a company whose products maintain their volume of sales, or even increase volume may become complacent and fail to recognise its relative decline in the market as a whole, as indicated in Fig. 54.

This decline in company share is usually attributed to a

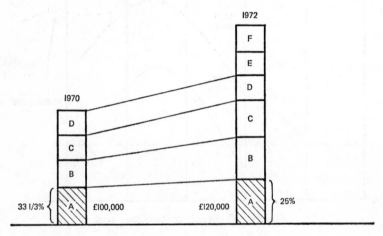

FIG. 54.—*The company and market share.*
1970. Sales of product A–£100,000; share of market—⅓.
1972. Sales of product A–£120,000: increase in sales—20%;
but share of market—¼.

failure to recognise the need for product change soon enough, or a failure to maintain a percentage share of the market. To avoid such a situation a company will conduct regular market research surveys to ascertain that their successful products are not losing ground to competitors. In the expanding market to stay in the same place requires increased effort, while to increase their market share may involve a company in an unacceptably high level of selling and distribution costs. At this time we are not, unfortunately, in an expanding market, but even so, vigilance must prevail over complacency. There is a great temptation under such circumstances to indulge in a knock-down fight with competitors for market share, especially on the international level. It is not the answer as it only results in a generally lower level of profitability all round. What is needed is an awareness of changing patterns of consumer demand that should be reflected in the company's product policy.

Marketing is not simply a strategy for economic growth, as in recession the companies that survive will be the ones that understand their customers and respond correctly in terms of product policy and service.

Whether products are successful refinements of some original idea, or whether they are completely new products necessitating changes in production and skills, the results must be seen in terms of profitability. To determine the right level of profit, in line with company plans in the longer term, is a task of management. Only by a planned and continuous product policy can these objectives be achieved.

CHAPTER NINE

Marketing analysis and forecasting

Market planning

Planning is one of the elements of management and is basic to any management activity since any process of work must begin with planning. In marketing, planning must precede the sequence of work whether marketing research, sales force or distribution. Planning, however, is not concerned solely with operational needs but is deeply concerned with the determination of the overall company strategy. The lesser objectives relating to departmental objectives and individual goals permitting management by objectives will be derived from the corporate strategy.

Any firm or marketing department will, in preparing its business plans, first prepare a tentative objective. It happens that the investigation to formulate the plan may produce information that will decide management against further development.

Firms which have analysed their strategy and worked to predetermined objectives over several years will review their current objectives in the light of experience. This may lead to a review of their performance and produce a tentative current objective. From this a current forecast will be made with the purpose of major objectives. The current forecast will have been developed from the process of long-range planning.

If a company has not previously prepared plans on the basis of strategic analysis it may find difficulty in coming to an explicit objective for the first time. Having no previous experience in long-range planning, the company must start by examining its past performance and extrapolating this into the future. This can be weighted to account for factors which will create deviations from the extrapolated trend. The need for strategic analysis and forecasting often arises from disturbances in established trends caused by changes in the company's environment. Threat

By comparing the determined objectives with the current forecast it is possible to measure the gaps, which is the discrepancy between what the firm wants (to achieve other goals) and what it is likely to achieve.

A company may aim for 10 per cent growth in sales during the coming two years, with a $2\frac{1}{2}$ per cent increase in market share. When it has completed its current forecast it finds that one of its major products is not likely to achieve anticipated sales due to technological developments. The gap has to be made up, either by expanding sales of other products, or by introducing a new product (*see* Fig. 55). In these circumstances the company may decide to introduce a new product to make up for the one that is failing, in which case a new set of forecasts will be needed.

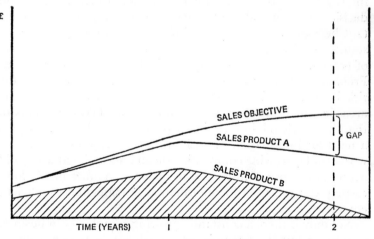

FIG. 55.—*Gap between objectives and forecast sales.*

The existence of such a gap will necessitate revised objectives, depending on the nature of the gap. If expectations exceed the objective, this may be adjusted upwards.

The determination of corporate policy implies that the organisation must ensure that it is both logical and attainable and that the subsequent objectives are realistic and in line with the company's skills and resources. To make sure that this is so the company has important information needs which have to be fulfilled by technical, marketing and economic research. Companies operate under conditions in which change is rapid through technological innovations and discoveries, exploitation of new resources, experience and the increasingly complex environment in which product development is both extended and costly. A company committed to a policy extended over several years must endeavour to predict the likely return on its investment over a period of time. It can only do this if it is in continuing contact with its environment through marketing research and extends this into the future through the process of forecasting.

The forecasting problem

As businesses grow in size and complexity, so the needs for information also grow. The information is required to aid decision-making and the greater the decision the more important becomes the demand for information. Managers are constantly faced with decision-making and to minimise the degree of error it is necessary to systematically predict likely events. Problems can arise in many areas but it is possible to reduce the risk by determining clear objectives and then analysing the areas in which problems will possibly occur, taking the maxim that the problem is implicit in the policy. There has always been a need for information in business but the rapid expansion of world trade, growing competition on an international scale, and a very real sense of insecurity in major economies makes forecasting and the need for information fundamental to efficient enterprise.

Not only is there a constantly growing complexity in business operations but the dynamics of growth are themselves complicated. Firms are continually expanding as they seek to optimise their use of resources. To operate, firms need services, plant and operating facilities, skilled operatives, managers and new research, but to obtain these they must buy resources in the form of land and buildings, a labour force or research scientists. Since the firm can only buy resources in discreet quantities it has a continual necessity to grow in order to optimise operations.

Marketing management appoints a salesman to a territory

hitherto unexploited, *i.e.* an export market. The salesman develops a high volume of sales which calls into being additional production. The extra production creates the need for overtime working and then increased production facilities which in turn leads to a need to expand the warehouse. Now marketing finds it has to expand sales to fully utilise the increased output and so it goes on. It is this continual need to optimise a whole that inevitably leaves some resource under-utilised that is at the root of growth dynamics (*see* Fig. 56).

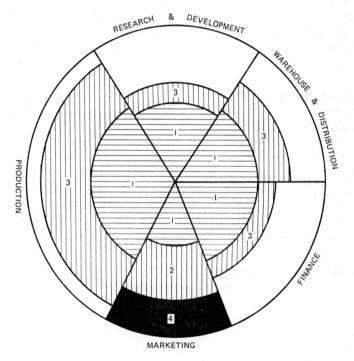

FIG. 56.—*Resource optimisation and growth.*

Such growth is frequently possible only by diversification, expansion, merger or acquisition, and these in turn within the frameworks imposed by government, technical change and environmental development. It is not simply that change is taking place, but that it is happening at an ever-accelerating pace, and within the possibilities offered by new capabilities in communication. Greater decisions with far-reaching ramifications have to be taken even more quickly when the communication system is able to transmit the results, and the implications for competitors, around the world almost instantaneously. The role of forecasting in this situation is to enable management to identify this rapidly changing velocity of business and keep pace with it.

Enterprises now compete on the world scale of international marketing. The development of trading communities and a general expansion of the number of nations now engaged in world trade has greatly increased the competitive pressures, irrespective of whether a company operates internationally or only within its national boundaries. To compete adequately in this environment requires larger companies able to undertake the research that technology demands or competition necessitates. To avoid excessive costs, both in terms of finance and opportunity cost, management must be capable of planning to meet long-term objectives and forecasting offers essential guidance.

The central problem of forecasting is to predict consumer behaviour at some point in the future. To understand why consumer behaviour is important it is necessary to understand the way in which consumer goods are central to economic output. Consumer goods are bought by final consumers to satisfy their wants, their purchase is frequently based on irrational considerations and result from impulse buying, but their actions set in motion a chain of production that provides demand for capital goods. Capital goods are used by producers to produce consumer goods, *e.g.* a heavy moulding machine is needed to press out pop records. The chain of production has as its ultimate objective the satisfaction of a consumer need and this produces growth in the demand for producer's (capital) goods. Of course a decline in the demand for consumer goods results in a fall in the demand for capital goods. The central problem during a recession is to maintain enough consumer demand to avoid the fall in demand for capital goods which are generally produced by major employers. A fall in the demand for washing machines leads to a fall in demand for capital goods for their production and in turn a fall in the demand for steel. Aggregate the demand of all consumer goods requiring capital goods and then steel and a major industry is failing.

Firms in the consumer sector will readily understand such

trends and be able to identify them without too much difficulty. The firm in the industrial sector has special problems. Generally industrial producers deal with a small number of customers which makes it difficult to draw accurate conclusions on an overall trend since the population is too small. An industrial producer may be producing only a small part of a more complex process, or a single component in a finished article and is dependent upon the final producer for guidance on the future needs. This problem is typified by the troubles facing the motor cycle industry in Britain where the failure of one producer results in failure or short-time for its suppliers.

Companies operating under such uncertain conditions must of necessity make the forecasting of economic trends and business an essential first step to forecasting. Managers must take decisions based on such predictions about the future. When the information has been gathered it must be applied to the business operation.

Forecasting economic and general business conditions depends upon the collection of sufficiently relevant data allowing a forecast that will be realistic enough for forward prediction. In those companies which are affected to a major degree by the multiplier operating in the economy and as a consequence are subject to leverage, advantages will be obtained from an early identification of any downturn in the economy. This will aid them in avoiding a marked decrease in cash flows and the consequent payment of a high rate of interest. Businessmen can make use of many indicators that will guide them in their decision-making but it must be remembered it is rarely possible to apply economic statistics to an individual situation. Rational decisions related to turning points in the trade cycle can only be taken after a systematic evaluation of historic and current events which can be related to the company's situation.

It is the job of forecasting to provide information which will enable a firm to predict what might happen under certain future conditions. The distance the forecast extends into the future will be a characteristic of the forecast. However, for a forecast to be effective, in any time period, it must be a continuous process, always searching ahead for information for a time period of years, as shown in Fig. 57.

The long-range objective forecast has to identify the company's reason for existence in the long term. It will endeavour to keep

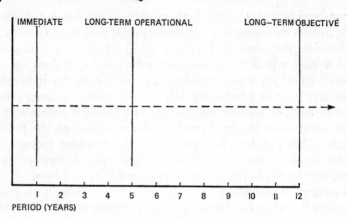

FIG. 57.—*Time periods in forecasting.*

executives alert to environmental changes that can affect their methods of operation and identify the need for change in their stated objectives.

The factors about which the forecast seeks information are in the areas of population dynamics, economic trends, technological discoveries and more than ever factors relating to socio-political change such as pollution and nationalisation. In undertaking this forecast the company seeks to systematically analyse its capabilities, marketing knowledge and skills in relation to identifiable future needs or changes. In this aligning of abilities on the one hand and environmental matters on the other the firm is asking itself the basic business questions about the reasons for its existence and its essential business purpose. The long-range objective forecast makes no pretence to accuracy and it seeks to identify the general changes which could by their occurrence affect the company's future operations.

Any firm in a complex technology industry faces long-term questions about the viability of its entire operation. In recent years the National Coal Board has involved itself in North Sea oil and Gulf Petroleum and Shell have both developed interests in nuclear power. All are due to changes in the energy field and the companies have seen the wisdom of a long-term concept of not limiting their potential to a traditional source of energy.

Many companies in industry, ranging from steel and brick producers to oil and motor manufacturers, have invested heavily in the prospects of under-water exploration for food, mineral wealth and energy sources. Fig. 30 in Chapter 5, the evolving corporate identity model, shows how firms may relate to much wider issues than they are currently involved in.

The aim of *the long-range operational forecast* is to shorten the time period to a span that represents the time lapse between identifying the need for change and the ability of the firm to do so. The type of product will determine the time needed; for example, a relatively simple production like clothing will be able to adapt fairly rapidly since the equipment is general in its use and not too specialised, whereas production of high technology output, such as aircraft, will use specific equipment and technology which is non-adaptable. Extending the problem to the extreme, the construction of nuclear power stations from design to completion may take fifteen years or more. Fig. 58 illustrates some of the complex influences on present-day operational plans.

In conditions where a firm is committed to an inflexible objective for many years, there has to be a continual appraisal of likely effects to alert the firm as soon as possible. The bases of information which will fulfil these information needs may be classified under two broad areas, economic and social.

The economic information will include the use of resources, population trends, levels of income, structure of industry and developments in trading organisations. The social information will relate to consumer trends and buying habits, the distribution of income and attitudes towards technological innovation. Only after careful selection of information needs, collection and analysis of facts can predictions be communicated to the operational areas of business and assist in decision-making.

The *short-range or immediate forecast* is concerned with the period in which decision-making is on a daily basis. A year is the usual period of the forecast and may be further divided into months or quarters. Since it is concerned with the immediate future and the information can be regarded as factual and reliable, the forecaster can aim for a high degree of accuracy in predicting the future. Much of the information is derived from salesmen's results and market research, or from production figures. The statistical base will be a historical record of the firm and, by extrapolation, described below, future demands can be indicated. From this information the necessary control system

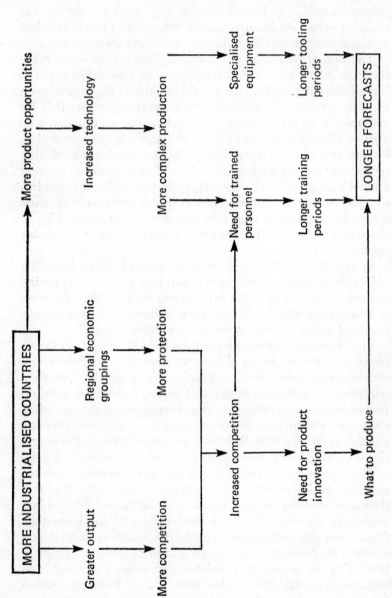

FIG. 58.—Factors in long-term operational forecasts.

can be built in to measure actual performance against predicted performance.

The basis of forecasting

The decision-maker is faced with a choice of techniques in his search for the right way to predict the future. It is possible to use one or a combination of several methods. In this choice he will be guided by two factors, the degree of accuracy and the cost of obtaining information. This was illustrated in Fig. 4, Chapter 2. The cost and accuracy increase with sophistication but may not always be justifiable. Against this, however, is the opportunity cost of not obtaining information, the cost of inaccuracy in terms of lost sales and/or wrong production.

There are four basic ways to forecast—informed opinion, internal information, market research and quantitative techniques.

Informed opinion can be used for the immediate forecast as it is concerned with short-term problems. Generally a manager can call upon opinion from customers and other businessmen. The main disadvantage is the likely unreliability but opinion may be tempered with knowledge and experience.

Any company will have collected over a period of years a great deal of information which correctly presented and analysed can provide a basis for prediction. The sources of such information lie in production figures, sales records, salesmen's records and accounting records. They provide a historical and factual record which can be used to detect trends. Users of such information should be aware, however, that the records, while explaining what happened frequently cannot show why it happened. Since the information is historical, it can logically refer only to the past and becomes outdated.

Marketing research is concerned with the present and seeks to understand and interpret very recent happenings. Because of this it is a more certain source of information from which forecasting can be attempted. Marketing research also embraces economic research, advertising research, consumer research and market research, all concerned with specific problems.

Industrial companies have particular problems in collecting data for research and in its subsequent interpretation:

"Like most large industrial companies, English China Clays is placing more emphasis on market research, forecasting and planning in order to understand and anticipate the requirements of the markets we serve. As a major supplier to the paper industry, which is by far the largest outlet for china clay, we decided some time ago to make ourselves more familiar with both the paper industry and the markets for its products."

The United Kingdom Market for Coated Printing Paper 1968–1974, English China Clays Sales Company Ltd.

A manufacturer of a consumer product is able to deal directly with his market through statistical techniques, but the industrial producer may be only one step in the long process of production. His market exists only because the finished product is demanded by consumers who are frequently at the end of a long distribution chain, and as buyers of the finished product may not even know that the industrial producer exists. To quote the above source from English China Clays again:

". . . the market is fragmented, diffuse and complex and subject to a whole variety of influences from publishers, printers, advertisers and major users. In the course of the survey we found that the influence of the paper maker tends to be passive rather than active and to originate more from production considerations than from marketing requirements."

As an example of the problems of the industrial producer English China Clays are far removed from the final product, but as their market research shows, very much aware of their dependency upon their ultimate consumers. Much of the output of English China Clays Ltd. is used for coating paper and to a high degree their function is bound up with the printing, travel, advertising and publishing business, themselves markets very susceptible to economic pressures. In 1968 an extensive market research project was entered into with the objective of forecasting demand until 1974. In discussing the structure of the market the following comment was made:

"In the course of the survey we found that the market for coated printing papers in the United Kingdom was complex, fragmented and subject to a variety of often conflicting influences."

To determine likely levels of demand by 1974 the English China Clays Sales Company Ltd. instituted an extensive survey into the demand from end-users of the product (*see* Table XV).

During the early years of the 1970s the U.K. market for consumer magazines and travel brochures in particular has contracted as a result of economic pressures. In West Germany, where general consumer magazines continue to have a wide appeal in a more affluent economy, the demand for coated papers has not been depressed.

TABLE XV. *Estimated end-use of coated printing papers.*

		000 tonnes
Publishing		
Trade and technical journals	66	
Consumer magazines	33	
Part publications	8	
Books and directories	20	
		127
Advertising		
Mail order catalogues	23	
Direct mail and trade catalogues	20	
Holiday and travel brochures	14	
Other advertising uses		
(mail shots, brochures, leaflets, etc.)	55	
		112
Labels and wrappers		40
Other uses		
House magazines, greeting cards, one-sided papers for sticking to packaging board, etc.		18
Total		297

Holiday and travel brochures in particular have been affected by the economic climate and they form a significant segment of the end-user market. English China Clays undertook extensive research into the demand from the holiday industry.

"Some of the large tour operators place greater emphasis on press and television advertising to persuade people to send for brochures. Brochure distribution is associated more closely with holidays abroad than those taken in this country, which are less likely to be organised."

The vast majority of holidays are taken in this country. Of

the five million who holidayed abroad in 1968 it has been estimated that at least two-and-a-half million were on holidays organised by tour operators. It has also been estimated by the trade that between ten and twelve brochures were produced for each booking.

Quantitative techniques

In recent years quantitative techniques have become important and in wider use. The reasons for their wider acceptance derive from the clearer interpretations which are possible when the variables can be quantified. In numerative terms the relationships between the variables are more readily understood and enable greater precision. Such precision can, however, only result from a clear interpretation of the assumptions on which the propositions are based.

The four main techniques used in quantitative forecasting are:

1. Moving averages;
2. extrapolation;
3. exponential smoothing;
4. correlation analysis.

Moving averages is a technique enabling a relationship to be easily seen between two sets of figures. One of these, usually the previous year, is historical and the other current. It is necessary to keep records over a period of months, exceeding one year. Such a table might be of sales as follows:

TABLE XVI. *Sales of product x, 1974.*

Month	Sales (£)	Moving average (£)
January	950	950
February	850	900
March	900	900
April	920	905
May	1,020	928
June	1,200	960
July	1,300	1,020
August	1,350	1,061.25
September	1,300	1,087.77
October	1,200	1,099
November	900	1,080.99
December	650	1,045

The moving average is obtained by adding the monthly totals and dividing by the number of months. Therefore, for August, the calculation is:

$$\text{Total sales, January–August } \frac{£8490}{8} = £1061.25$$

The technique is simple and provides an indication of how present performance compares with the previous year, and also shows the direction of the trend. If records extend over several years a better indication of trends will be available by comparing current figures with the corresponding period in previous years. This will enable seasonal variations to be taken into account.

Extrapolation is a forecasting technique which relies upon the projection of past trends. From examination of past sales a company may find its sales have been increasing by 5 per cent

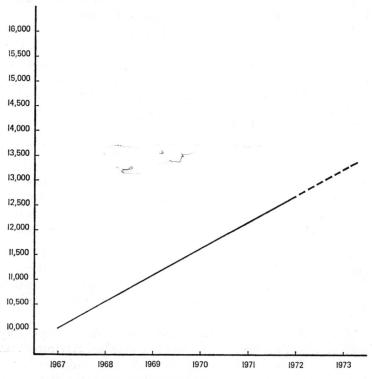

FIG. 59.—*Extrapolation at 5 per cent per year.*

per year. If the trend is evident over a number of years it will become possible to extend the trend into the next year, as in Fig. 59. The principal fault with extrapolation is that it is valid only in fairly static circumstances, as it does not take into account the possibility of unexpected competitive activity.

Extrapolation as a technique has its limitations and is most suited to those values which cannot be constructed from individual cases, or where investigation into the interacting relationships would be too long and costly. An accurate sales forecast might be influenced by population growth, increases in discretionary spending or population movements.

Exponential smoothing is a technique used in forecasting demand and is based upon recent levels of demand. It is necessary to take the moving average over a period of time, usually a short period, five or six months, since longer periods would tend to produce a too consistent average. The resultant moving averages are then projected as a trend showing likely levels in demand for a future period, as in Fig. 60.

Both moving averages and extrapolation are devoted to finding measures involving a single collection of figures. Frequently in business the forecaster is concerned with examining two variables. In this he is attempting to relate the two sets to see if one is in any degree determined by the other. Such a problem is illustrated below: the relationship between advertising expenditure and sales results.

Month	Advertising expenditure(£)	Sales(£)
May	1,000	25,000
June	2,500	45,000
July	2,000	30,000
August	3,000	40,000
September	1,500	35,000

The purpose of seeking such a relationship is to predict and control events. If a company can determine a close relationship between, say, advertising and sales it will be possible to predict just how much advertising will be needed to produce a given volume of sales.

The ability to predict one figure from another is especially useful if one of the figures is subject to a time lag. It is important for the forecaster to know which of the two variables is the independent variable and which is the dependent. The inde-

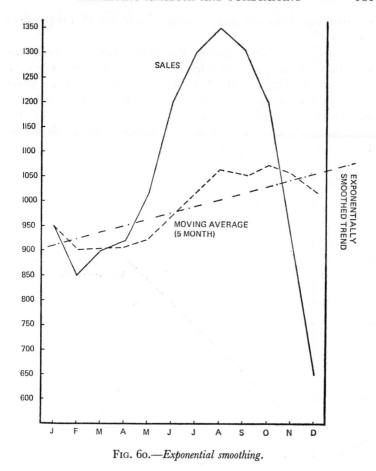

FIG. 60.—*Exponential smoothing.*

pendent variable is the one which is not affected by changes in the other variable. In the example given above it can be expected that alterations to the volume of advertising will be reflected in variations in the level of sales.

Conversely changes in sales volume will not have a direct effect on the level of advertising expenditure. Determining which is the dependent variable is not always a simple matter. Consumption of raw materials and levels of output represent two variables. If raw materials are scarce, then it will be the independent variable, for output will be decided by how much material is available. On the other hand, if output is determined by demand then the raw materials will be the dependent variable.

A method of determining the relationship between the variables advertising and sales, as in Fig. 61, is the use of a scattergraph. This is a graph with a scale for the two variables and on this scale the variable values are plotted. The method is to construct a graph with the independent variable along the horizontal axis and the dependent variable on the vertical axis. Each pair of figures is plotted as a point on the graph where the

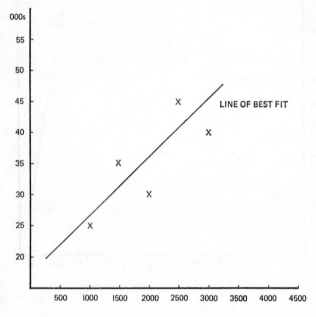

FIG. 61.—*Correlation analysis.*

two lines of the variables intersect. The May figure of £1,000 advertising and £25,000 sales will be plotted together. In this case a general rise is evident suggesting that as advertising expenditure increases sales volume rises, but it is not constant. To make the result a little clearer the values could be increased by a line of best fit which it is judged to fit the pattern best. This line is shown on Fig. 61.

It has been shown above how more complexity in business has created a need for longer and more accurate forecasting.

Many would argue that the problems that need to be solved in accurate forecasting outweigh the advantages to be gained. Many of the difficulties arise from lack of information upon which to base forecasts and, when it can be found, it may be unreliable. There may exist variables which are quite unpredictable to the average businessman, for instance the Arab–Israeli war of October 1973 which produced a crisis in oil and led to a downturn in economic growth in many countries. Other problems and margins of error arise from errors in interpretation and calculation in sophisticated techniques. Problems may also arise from changes in the macro-economy or in the suppliers or the customers of the firm.

G

CHAPTER TEN

Analysis and control
of the selling organisation

In Chapter 1 it was suggested that many older marketing men, especially those who originated in the purely selling function, tend to pragmatism rather than scientific enquiry. While the marketing function certainly influences this purely practical approach by its need for analysis and research, it is still a frequent criticism of sales management that it is insufficiently scientific in its decision-making. There is a tendency for sales management to pursue volume rather than profitability or productivity. This often arises out of a failure to plan on a comprehensive basis, relying on hunch and intuition where techniques of measurement may offer a more positive guide.

It should not be thought that this is undue criticism, after all sales management operates in the least controllable area of business. Marketing as a function is concerned with customers but it can influence the market through its activities of advertising and communications generally and seeks to understand the market through its research activities. Sales management, as a sub-function of the total marketing function, is much closer to and dependent upon the customer. Whereas marketing as a whole is concerned with customers as segments, or groups, sales management is much more concerned with customers as individuals and therefore is to a greater extent influenced by their idiosyncrasies. It is very probably true to say that there is an area of misunderstanding between the marketing man and the sales manager arising out of this relationship to the customer.

In the field of industrial selling, the performance of the sales force is without doubt the most important element in the marketing-mix and the biggest contributor to success. The other tools of marketing communications, advertising, sales promotion and

184

even competition pricing cannot pull goods into consumption with the impact of the sales force. Industrial buying decisions are rational and based upon cost/benefit considerations instead of emotional appeals. Often they require a considerable element of advice and even a service in the form of analysis of a customer's problems and a suggested solution.

The sales organisation is a complicated system which is influenced by many variables which often prove difficult to quantify and produce unpredictable interactions. The sales force, as an activity of the sub-function of sales management, is interposed between the company and the customer and fills a role best described as two-way representation. The communications aspect of the salesman's job is often under-emphasised and overshadowed by its selling tasks. This of course should be so, as the fundamental purpose of the sales force is to *sell* the company's goods or services. Nevertheless increasingly the sales force is becoming a channel of communication between company and customer, supplying information to the firm about the customer and the market requirements and supplying the customer with information about the company's goods and services.

Fig. 62 is reproduced from the author's book, *Sales and Sales Management*, Macdonald & Evans, 1973, and shows the two-way tasks of the salesman and his responsibilities. The salesman frequently has to be a devil's advocate when his company proposes changes which the salesman believes to be against the best interest of his customer and, in the long term, his company.

At the root of much of sales management's problems directly associated with the sales force is the question of compensation and status. Traditionally salesmen have been paid on the basis of salary plus commission on sales. This system of compensation has several faults. It tends to attract people anxious to earn high incomes, often at any cost. By this is meant a situation in which a salesman is attracted to the selling job by the prospects of high income, but which in turn tends to produce volume sales of short-term business rather than planned sales. The difference lies in the longer-term results since the salesman who is drawn by income considerations alone tends to be less responsible in his obtaining of orders. Frequently he makes high volume sales from a large number of small, trial orders and then moves on. Unfortunately this often leads to bad relations

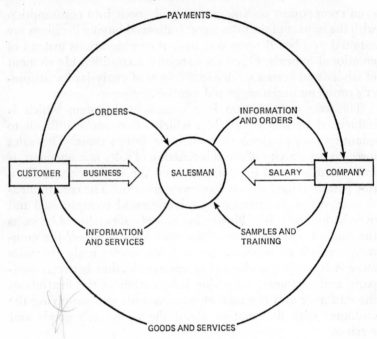

FIG. 62.—*Two-way communication model.*

between the customer and the company arising from misuse of products.

Sales management has a task in this area to devise systems of compensation that remove this attitude of selling volume orders in terms of easy selling but low profit items. If compensation is of a level that gives the salesman status and an income in line with the general trend of industry incomes it can lead to planned sales effort and judicious territory management. But, the hard-liners argue, what is to prevent a salesman then putting little effort into the job, if he is not subject to carrot and stick controls? The answer lies in management taking greater care in its recruitment and training programmes. For example:

1. Greater attention to the job specification resulting from careful job analysis.
2. More attention in the selection of sales personnel.
3. Provision of sensible induction training and then continuous training programmes.
4. Providing a work situation permitting greater motiva-

tion arising from improving the salesman's status and allowing him more control of his own activities by providing
sensible and attainable objectives.

5. Ensuring that company policies and products are based
on continuous marketing research.

Motivation is fundamental to achieving good performance
from the sales force and sales management has a prime responsibility to see that conditions of work enable the self-motivated
salesman to succeed while working within the policy of the
company. The performance aspects of this have been dealt with
in greater detail in Chapter 7.

All management should be seen as a whole even if at times we
are obliged to study or apply it piecemeal. In effective sales
organisations it is management's ability to combine all its tools,
skills and experience that enable it to meet the declared objectives that is the common denominator. The ability of the sales
force to sell creatively is largely determined by management's
product policy and implemented by ensuring it has the correct
product at the right time and the creation of logical channels
of distribution. This entirety of management's task necessitates
looking at the whole range of activities as a system.

A system is a set of interacting variables which in marketing
usage must be regarded as an open system because the variables
are never constant. New variables enter the system and the old
variables leave it as economic and marketing factors change.
Fig. 63 is a model of the marketing system and within this is the
sub-function of sales management.

An organised behaviour system such as the sales organisation
must be purposeful and the ends to which it aims are called
goals. A sales organisation will, in the course of its work, have
many different goals, frequently at the same time. It may aim
for efficiency, lower costs, greater sales volume, better training,
lower manpower replacement and each of these goals will be
more or less important than others. Sales management's task
in this respect is to *sub-optimise* these goals but to avoid a maximisation of one at the expense of the others. These goals will
themselves be derived from the interaction of the variables
and because of the complexity and range of the independent
variables in the environment of the sales organisation sub-
function, it is helpful to apply the *systems concept*.

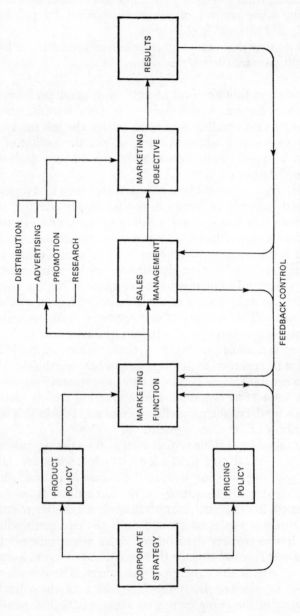

FIG. 63.—Marketing system and sales management sub-function.

Systems concept in sales management

Systems engineering, like operational research, orginated to meet the needs of novel military situations during World War Two. Following the war, the pressures of complex engineering and technological problems concerned with nuclear power and the space programme developed the total systems concept into a highly mathematical subject. Sales management can utilise the principles of systems engineering to aid its problem-solving and increase the department's poductivity.

A system comprises a variety of inputs making up a process which in turn produces a measurable output. The measurement in sales management represents a feedback of information permitting a control on the inputs in order to meet an objective. In terms of sales management the system of concern is the sales organisation and reference again to Fig. 63 will aid understanding.

The inputs to the system are the marketing objectives, *i.e.*, the product and pricing policies which will be determined by corporate strategy, and the resources which are to be committed to achieve the marketing objectives. Inputs to the system become determinants of the process and will be reflected in the selection of the marketing-mix and its application in terms of other activities and tasks. Finally the output is measured.

An essential of any system is the provision of feedback information to tell top management what has happened and why, and whether their overall strategy should be changed as a result. Fig. 64 illustrates the way in which continual feedback monitors performance and produces adaptations to strategy. The measurement of output is a basic necessity of a system approach as it provides the means of control. This may be measured in terms of the return on investment, contribution to corporate growth, market share or profitability of the operation.

The sales force is a semi-autonomous unit within the larger sales organisation sub-function. The kind of output measurement described above, while an effective measure of the overall company, is too much outside the control of the sales force. Some other measures have to be employed to show how the sales force is operating. There are five possible measures of sales

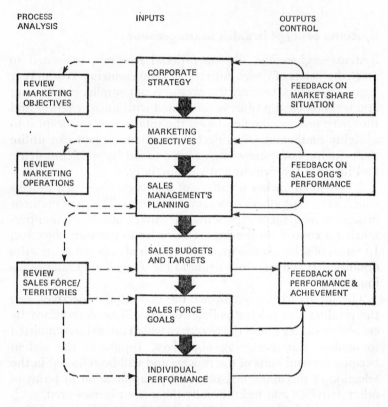

PROCESS
ANALYSIS

INPUTS

OUTPUTS
CONTROL

FIG. 64.—*Feedback control in sales management.*

force productivity, by which a comparison can be made with other forces:

1. *Contribution to profit.* Production, on completion, is made over to the sales organisation at cost, and is in turn sold at a price representing total costs, including profit. The additional cost of selling and distribution has to be covered by a mark-up and is the sales force's contribution to corporate profit.

2. *Sales cost ratio.* Sales expenses divided by sales volume provides a ratio for measuring performance against the cost of achieving it. It has to be used in conjunction with other measures, especially marginal considerations, to relate performance to market size, since a sales force selling £1 million at 5

per cent expense/volume ratio may not be as profitable as one selling £5 million at 7 per cent cost ratio.

3. *Return on assets employed.* A sales force is far more than an organisation of persons. Sales personnel are generally supplied with cars, they have to be supported with samples, literature and an office organisation. Money has to be invested in warehousing and stock and in outstanding accounts. If the current expenditure on salesmen's salaries and travel are subtracted from gross profit and sales volume the balance will be the return on the capital assets employed.

4. *Achievement of marketing objectives.* A sales organisation operates within the constraints of marketing objectives. These objectives will result from marketing analysis and forecasting and will present sales with quantifiable goals. Achievement of these goals will represent a measure of performance by the sales force. Such objectives by marketing, such as an increase in market share by 10 per cent, will be measurable goals for the sales force and should also determine what profitability is demanded and so put an expenditure constraint on sales as well as a performance control.

5. *Share of market.* It is not easy to relate market share to a standard of performance since the sales force will be only one variable among many. The level of advertising, pricing policy, quality standard and product policy will also be influential variables. In addition the activities of competitors will have a strong influence on market share, especially if the sales force is not supported by an active marketing function.

The application of the systems concept to a sales management problem follows seven stages of analysis:

1. Define the purpose of the system to be analysed.
2. Define the objectives of the system.
3. Quantify the relationships within the system; what inputs are required?
4. Determine the measurable performance or outputs of each element.
5. Evaluate in terms of costs/benefits alternative solutions to the system and their constraints.
6. Implement the "best" solution; what is the efficiency of the organisation relating output to input?

7. Determine the feedback control process to monitor results.

In practical terms the analysis would follow a process along the lines of the following example, a problem involving breaking into the West German market for menswear.

1. Define the system.

The market for men's suits in Western Germany.

2. Define the objectives of the system.

To provide a bulk market for top quality men's suits, distributed through department stores, supported by media advertising. Market = % of total market for B- and C-rated consumers.

3. Quantify the relationships within the system.

What are the buying habits of male consumers in West Germany? How many potential customers; where do they buy; how much do they pay; what influences styling, colour, design; what is their likely reaction to British clothing; what sort of quantities are involved; how can we ship them?

4. Determine the measurable performance of each element.

To achieve the objectives, what is required of the products, distribution system, promotional aids, discount structures, personal selling, buying times, exhibitions?

5. Evaluate costs/benefits of alternative systems.

Analyse effectiveness of appointing agents/representatives selling to other outlets. What costs in salary and commissions; expenses; what are the contractual requirements; do we need a warehouse; who pays for despatch, etc.?

salesmen to make more calls each week or management may increase the total number of salesmen. There is a limit to the profitability of increasing the size of the sales force as beyond a certain point the sales force will be pursuing marginal sales potential.

How much effort is being expended in achieving the sales force's results indicates whether the quality of the sales calls and the effectiveness of presentation are being maximised. This input is measured by the calls/order ratio, the value of each order and its profitability, or the number of calls that result from pursuing specific objectives rather than windfall orders.

Management can ensure that effort is maximised by training programmes that stress the need for salesmen to analyse their own operations. To do this efficiently the salesman must have guidelines to help him decide priorities, including: (a) which key activities will lead to increased selling success, *i.e.* product story, follow-up of enquiries, preparing specifications in advance; (b) selling strategy, *i.e.* emphasis on product reliability, performance or savings that will be achieved.

In industrial selling this measurement is not as simple a matter as it might be in measuring calls on grocers' shops. Frequently industrial selling involves many non-selling calls in order to win approval, seek information or ensure products are specified for long-term projects. In the same way these industrial calls also involve a salesman making several calls to solve problems, work out details of treatments or the type of equipment needed. This aspect of the salesman's inputs is one that can be influenced a great deal by improved induction training and by a programme of continuous training.

The third input, the productivity of the methods employed, analyses whether salesmen allocate their time sufficiently between maintaining existing business and creating new business. For each sales territory and salesman there is some optimum frequency for calling on different sizes and categories of customers. The industrial sales problem exemplifies the need to allocate time. Calls on architects and consulting engineers rarely produce orders and if a salesman spends too much time with this category of customers, his short-term volume will suffer, but if he ignores them altogether long-term business will be less certain.

Management's control of the system derives from the range

of control variables. These can be varied in the intensity of their application and their combination to achieve sales objectives. The selection of the variables will result from analysing the needs of the sales organisation and modified when necessary in the light of performance achieved and reported by the feedback process. In particular management must provide guidance on such matters as:

1. Which sales problems deserve attention and how time should be allocated in the most constructive way.

2. How to make territory or market analyses to determine potential.

3. Evaluation of selling requirements for existing and potential business.

Sales management may establish budgets to measure and control the sales force's output variables. It is difficult, however, to establish such quantifiable goals for the range of salesmen's inputs without imposing constraints upon the salesman. These goals are usually in terms of the number of calls, where the calls should be and the ratio of calls to orders. The conscientious salesman, who is well motivated, will resent the degree of planning this approach necessitates and will emphasise that quality of calls is equally important to the number of calls.

The systems approach to increasing sales force productivity requires the sales manager to establish the flow chart by determining improvement objectives. He then traces the flow backwards through the salesman's outputs and inputs to determine what changes are needed in the range of control variables. An objective to reduce the cost of sales will lead management to consider changes in organisation, territories, training, compensation and planning.

Generally analysis will lead to the improvement of several control variables and in determining what these should be and what resources should be employed to bring about the desired change management is faced with four questions.

1. What is the relationship between the control variables and the salesman's input variable that is to be changed? If the control variable has a low relationship to the input variable it may be omitted from our considerations. The remainder are analysed according to the needs of the firm, and

weighted to stress their importance in fulfilling a specific objective.

2. What level of performance should be expected from the control variable? It is helpful to establish standard performance ratings for the control variables and for the saleman's inputs. This makes an objective analysis feasible and forces management to focus attention on each variable in turn. This establishes two measures: the standard performance rating is a judgment of performance and the weighting is a judgment of the variable's importance in a situation.

3. How much would it cost to improve performance? The concept of diminishing marginal returns is useful here to understand that the better the performance is, the more costly it will be to improve performance further. Beyond a certain point, still further improvements can be achieved only at great expense.

4. How much would the productivity of the sales force be improved by increasing the efficiency of the variable? Sales management has to predict what the increase in productivity will mean in terms of net profitability, after the cost of introducing the improvement in the variable, *i.e.* more training.

Marginal analysis of selling costs

With economic models it is possible to show the effects of different expenditures, in terms of advertising, promotion and sales, on the firm's profits and sales volume in alternative market situations. The basic purpose of selling costs is to increase demand for the product, and they may be regarded as alternatives to price reductions as a strategy for expanding sales.

The important concept in decisions on the choice of strategy is the relative elasticities of promotion and price. If promotional elasticity is high while price elasticity remains low, the company is likely to adopt a policy of selling costs in preference to price cuts to expand sales. If price elasticity is higher then price cuts will achieve the objective of expanding sales more readily.

Marketing decisions which involve alternative strategies, such as choice of advertising or the sales force, apply the criterion, which solution is likely to yield maximum profits?

Expenditure on the sales force is based on two premises: (*a*)

that it will increase the costs of the firm; (*b*) successful application will increase the revenue of the firm. The decision on how
much to spend is one of equating the marginal cost of the sales
force with the marginal revenue.

Marginal analysis expresses certain relationships, *e.g.* that
an increase in selling cost is acceptable if there is an equal or
greater resulting increase in sales revenue. In practice it is
not so simple to determine what is happening, especially in the
short term. An increased expenditure on the sales force through
better training is not easy to equate in terms of improved selling
in the short term, although in the long term a better trained and
qualified sales force will *probably* result in higher sales revenues.
Any expenditures and results are difficult to isolate and measure
and the usual statistical problems of identification will be
encountered.

Another important consideration to be borne in mind in this
type of analysis is the influence of competitive activity, which
will be in evidence in any oligopolistic market.

What return on the investment?

Any business activity is basically about priorities. The criterion,
as discussed above, is the return on investment and marketing
management's basic problem is the need to calculate this.

In Chapter 3, regarding international decisions, it was stressed
that investment in international markets is only justifiable on
the premise that there is no better way available of securing a
return on the investment. Spending money on the sales force
involves the same choice. Such a decision has to be taken by
top management in possession of all the information on
alternative forms of investment. It is up to sales management
to justify the expenditure in terms of the predicted return.
It may be that there are other ways of achieving a sales objective other than increasing the size of the sales organisation. The
menswear manufacturer, Strads International, formerly had a
large national sales force and a system of overseas representation
selling to hundreds of accounts. In the early 1970s a new form
of selling was introduced when the firm began to sell their
products direct to the public through their own discount shops.
This resulted in reduced expenditure on a sales force, a closer

attained with fifteen salesmen (marked with an * on Table XVII) and represents an industrial selling situation where the sales-

TABLE XVII. *Size of sales force and contribution.*

Size of sales force	Total cost of sales force at £3,000 each	Penetration of market (%)	Sales in £1m market	25% contri-bution	Net contri-bution
25	75,000	65	650,000	162,500	87,500
22	66,000	63	630,000	157,500	91,500
20	60,000	60	600,000	150,000	90,000
15	45,000	55	550,000	137,500	92,500*
12	36,000	47	470,000	117,500	81,500
10	30,000	40	400,000	100,000	70,000

man is particularly effective due to the high priority for advice and information. The selling of fast-moving consumer goods would present a different situation as the purchasing behaviour of buyers is influenced to a high degree by advertising and sales promotion. Such a marketing-mix would present a very different cost/benefit structure and account would have to be taken of the long-term effects of advertising.

Use of method study in sales management

In Chapter 1 method study concepts were introduced as aids in marketing analysis and control. One of the areas in which they can be employed to improve efficiency and control of performance, is in the workings of the sales force. There are of course many variables, some would argue too many, to enable method study to be applied with the precision possible in the factory, where the jobs may be repetitive. Nevertheless its use as a technique is to improve performance, not make it perfect.

The T.U.C., in a publication of June 1963, *Outline of Work Study and payments by results* defined method study thus:

"Method study is the application of a *logical* procedure of investigation, in a form *suited* to the situation being studied." (The italics are mine.)

Method study is concerned with productivity and in analys-ing and controlling the marketing effort it accords with our objectives. Productivity is definable in terms of three results of work as was shown in Fig. 65.

1. *Utilisation*. To what extent do we utilise our sales force during the paid hours at their job?

2. *Effort*. To what extent is the sales force being utilised at their job; what effort is being expended?

3. *Method*. While the sales force is being utilised at their job, how efficient is the method being employed? Do salesmen work perfectly, well enough, or in a personalised "make-do" way?

The problem can be expressed in a simple formula:

$$P = a \times b \times c$$

where P is performance, a = utilisation, b = effort, c = method.

To clarify this, let us consider a salesman on an average day's selling. During an eight-hour day he *utilises* 60 per cent of his time in actual selling. On this basis he is *selling* for 4·8 hours and the remaining 3·2 hours is spent in travelling, rest periods, waiting to see people, etc. If during the actual *selling time* his *effort* is 75 per cent (using 100 as a standard performance), then the 4·8 hours of utilisation is further reduced to 3·4 hours, the remaining time he spends in casual conversation unrelated to the selling process. An examination of his *methods* in terms of presentation and expertise will reduce his overall performance yet again. Assuming his method averages 80 per cent of a standard performance rating the 3·4 hours falls to something like 2·7 hours of *productive* selling. In this example a = 60 per cent, b = 75 per cent, c = 80 per cent; therefore:

$$P = (60\%) \times (75\%) \times (80\%) = 36 \cdot 0\%$$

from a productivity target of 100.

There is an area of 64 per cent in which improvement and cost reduction is possible. The problem facing us is how do we measure and control a sales force of twenty men of different abilities in different territories?

The areas of difference are not really the problems since we must concern ourselves with the areas of similarity which can be treated logically and are within the framework of management's control variables.

Efficient training on a continuous basis will do much to

improve the techniques of doing the job: training in the use of the products; ensuring salesmen thoroughly understand their products and how to use them; training in the mechanics of doing the job—paperwork, report writing, making appointments, territory management; and all control variables that sales management can use to improve performance. This is not trying to remove the individuality of the work since salesmen tend to be individualists and it is important to retain the personalised aspects that are motivations.

Professor Frederick Hertzberg identified the fundamental problem by distinguishing different factors, which he termed "hygiene factors" and "motivators." These are dealt with in more detail in Chapter 7, but to recap, he saw hygiene factors as being those which prevent a worker from being unhappy, although they do not make him happy. It is what a man does that makes him happy and creates a work situation in which motivation is possible.

In the control of the sales force, product knowledge, territorial management and paperwork are hygiene factors affecting the conditions of work. It is sales management's task to evolve ways in which these routine but necessary aspects of the salesman's job can be made more hygienic. Only when that is achieved can the salesman get down to the job satisfaction and motivation element.

Method study, by examining the job and asking questions about why a certain job is done, can provide a climate for better understanding of the job and often free the salesman from many irksome problems.

A company selling industrial coatings required its salesmen to complete a weekly return on short- and long-term prospects. Each week salesmen would feel obliged to give details of schemes which would one day materialise. Analysis showed that in most instances the "prospects" were based on the flimsiest evidence but for the security of their jobs the salesmen felt that they had to put something down. This revealed not only the basic unhappiness and insecurity of the sales force, but also that the company was basing its forward production planning on information that was almost wholly unreliable.

Using standard method study symbols, slightly "bent" to a saleman's job instead of the shop floor, it is possible to illustrate a series of events during a typical day. The symbols are:

Operation; indicates main step in selling task, *i.e.* productive selling.

Inspection; indicates a check for quantity and/or quality, *i.e.* examining job.

Transportation; indicates the movement of worker, *i.e.* travelling from one customer to another or about the client's plant.

Delay; indicates a delay in sequence of events, *i.e.* waiting at customer's office, due to lack of fixed appointment.

Storage; indicates that material is being deliberately stored, *i.e.* report writing.

A series of events in the salesman's day can now be created linking the symbols to show what happened:

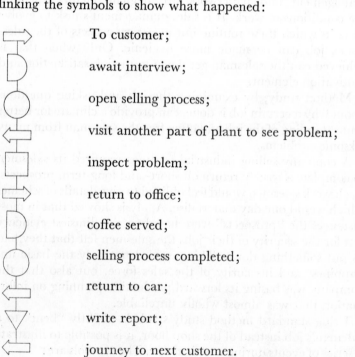

To customer;

await interview;

open selling process;

visit another part of plant to see problem;

inspect problem;

return to office;

coffee served;

selling process completed;

return to car;

write report;

journey to next customer.

If one extends this for the entire day the number of "o"s in relation to the other symbols would be very low while the number of symbols representing travelling time, coffee breaks, casual conversation and report writing would shock the average sales manager who has not analysed how his force utilise the eight-hour day.

The outcome of such a scientific analysis must be to avoid delays and wasted time by better training and supervision. Delays can be avoided by making appointments whenever possible or reasonable to do so. Better utilisation of time can result from analyses of territories and arranging journeys to meet an optimum number of customers per day, consistent with the time needed to do a good selling job. Ensuring the sales force is kept up to standard in terms of product and technology, knowledge will result in better specifications and quicker assessment of customers' problems. Salesmen should receive training in communication and report writing to avoid unnecessary "bumf" and to make the most of management by exception, that is, "if everything is alright don't tell me."

Appendix: Bibliography

ALDERSON, W.: *Dynamic marketing behaviour*, Irwin, 1965.

ALEXANDER & BERG: *Dynamic management in marketing*, Irwin, 1965.

ALEXANDER, CROSS & HILL: *Industrial marketing*, Irwin, 1967.

ALLEN, P.: *Sales and sales management*, Macdonald & Evans, 1973.

ALLEN, P.: *The practice of exporting*, Macdonald & Evans, 1975.

ANSOFF, H. I.: *Corporate strategy*, Pelican, 1968.

BRECH, E. F. L.: *The principles and practice of management*, Longmans, 1963.

BROWN, J. A. C.: *The social psychology of industry*, Pelican, 1962.

CURRIE, R. M.: *Work study*, Pitman, 1963.

FISK, G.: *Marketing systems, an introductory analysis*, Harper, 1967.

FOSTER, D. W.: *Planning for products and markets*, Longmans, 1972.

KOTLER, P.: *Marketing management, analysis, planning & control*, Prentice-Hall, 1972.

LONSDALE, J. E.: *Selling to industry*, Business Publications, 1966.

McGREGOR, D.: *Leadership and motivation*, M. I. T. Press, 1966.

McGREGOR, D.: *The human side of enterprise*, McGraw-Hill, 1960.

MORRELL, J.: *Management decisions & the role of forecasting*, Pelican, 1972.

PEARCE, C.: *Prediction techniques for marketing planners*, Associated Business Programmes, 1971.

SKINNER, R. N.: *Launching new products in competitive markets*, Cassell, 1972

THOMAS, M. J.: *International marketing management*, Houghton Mifflin, 1969.

TOMLINSON, R. C.: *O.R. comes of age*, Tavistock Publications, 1971.

Index